DIVISION OF NARCOTIC DRUGS
Vienna

DECLARATION OF THE INTERNATIONAL CONFERENCE ON DRUG ABUSE AND ILLICIT TRAFFICKING

AND

COMPREHENSIVE MULTIDISCIPLINARY OUTLINE OF FUTURE ACTIVITIES IN DRUG ABUSE CONTROL

UNITED NATIONS
New York, 1988

NOTE

Symbols of United Nations documents are composed of capital letters combined with figures. Mention of such a symbol indicates a reference to a United Nations document.

Material in this publication may be freely quoted or reprinted, but acknowledgement is requested, together with a copy of the publication containing the quotation or reprint.

ST/NAR/14

UNITED NATIONS PUBLICATION
Sales No. E.88.XI.1
ISBN 92-1-148075-2
00900P

Preface

The International Conference on Drug Abuse and Illicit Trafficking was convened at Vienna from 17 to 26 June 1987 as an expression of the political will of nations to combat the drug menace on a world-wide basis. The General Assembly, in its resolution 40/122 of 13 December 1985, gave the Conference a mandate "to generate universal action to combat the drug problem in all its forms at the national, regional and international levels". Transcending the traditional concerns of the international community with the control of the supply of narcotic drugs and psychotropic substances and of the illicit traffic in drugs, the Conference made a major breakthrough by deciding that a balanced approach was needed to deal with this plague affecting society and that the prevention of drug abuse and treatment and the rehabilitation of drug abusers should be accorded the same importance in policy and in action as the reduction of supply and illicit traffic.

The concept of a balanced approach is the key to the two main documents which emerged from the Conference, as representatives of 138 States were joined by representatives of a wide range of intergovernmental and regional organizations, nearly 200 non-governmental organizations and various entities and programmes of the United Nations system in a concerted attack on all aspects of the scourge of drug abuse.

The Declaration unanimously adopted by the Conference reaffirms the political will of the participating States to fight the drug problem and to commit themselves to vigorous international action against drug abuse and illicit trafficking. It sets forth suggested priorities for action and emphasizes the pivotal role of Governments in developing appropriate national strategies within which measures to strengthen international co-operation can be developed and recognizes the constant, determined efforts of Governments at the national, regional and international levels to counter the escalating incidence of drug abuse and illicit trafficking. The Declaration recognizes the important role of the United Nations system in the efforts to combat drug abuse and illicit trafficking. In addition, the significant role played by non-governmental organizations in the drive against drug abuse is recognized, and initiatives to strengthen the efforts of these organizations are encouraged.

The Comprehensive Multidisciplinary Outline of Future Activities in Drug Abuse Control, also adopted unanimously by the Conference, is a compendium of practical action for Governments, the United Nations system, intergovernmental and regional organizations, non-governmental organizations, academic institutions and individuals to take in combating drug abuse and illicit trafficking. In its four chapters, 35 action targets are set that are realistically attainable over the next 10-15 years, existing problems are defined and a course of action designed to attain these objectives is suggested.

The General Assembly of the United Nations welcomed the successful conclusion of the International Conference on Drug Abuse and Illicit Trafficking when it considered the report of the Conference in November 1987, and, in its resolution 42/112 of 7 December 1987, affirmed its commitment to the Declaration adopted by the Conference. The Assembly also urged Governments and organizations to take due account in the formulation of their programmes of the framework provided by the Comprehensive Multidisciplinary Outline of Future Activities in Drug Abuse Control, as a repertory of recommendations setting forth practical measures that can contribute to the fight against drug abuse and illicit trafficking.

The present publication is issued in response to the request of the General Assembly that adequate copies of the Declaration and of the Outline of Future Activities should be made available. It will be published in each of the six official languages of the United Nations: Arabic, Chinese, English, French, Russian and Spanish.

The index contains keywords used in the Outline of Future Activities and can serve as a reference guide to the relevant paragraphs, chapters and targets. It also includes references to the organizations, agencies and programmes mentioned in the text of the Outline.

CONTENTS

			Page
Preface			iii
Explanatory notes			viii

PART ONE: DECLARATION OF THE INTERNATIONAL CONFERENCE ON DRUG ABUSE AND ILLICIT TRAFFICKING 1

PART TWO: COMPREHENSIVE MULTIDISCIPLINARY OUTLINE OF FUTURE ACTIVITIES IN DRUG ABUSE CONTROL 5

		Paragraphs	
Introduction		1-17	5

Chapter

I. PREVENTION AND REDUCTION OF THE ILLICIT DEMAND FOR NARCOTIC DRUGS AND PSYCHOTROPIC SUBSTANCES .... 18-122 | 11

Introduction		18-25	11
Target 1.	Assessment of the extent of drug misuse and abuse	26-42	12
Target 2.	Organization of comprehensive systems for the collection and evaluation of data	43-55	16
Target 3.	Prevention through education	56-73	18
Target 4.	Prevention of drug abuse in the workplace	74-84	22
Target 5.	Prevention programmes by civic, community and special interest groups and law enforcement agencies	85-96	23
Target 6.	Leisure-time activities in the service of the continuing campaign against drug abuse	97-104	26
Target 7.	Role of the media	105-122	27

II. CONTROL OF SUPPLY .... 123-222 | 31

Introduction		123-127	31
Target 8.	Strengthening of the international system of control of narcotic drugs and psychotropic substances	128-142	32
Target 9.	Rational use of pharmaceuticals containing narcotic drugs or psychotropic substances	143-157	35

Target 10. Strengthening the control of international movements of psychotropic substances 158-165 37

Target 11. Action related to the increase in the number of controlled psychotropic substances 166-172 39

Target 12. Control of the commercial movement of precursors, specific chemicals and equipment 173-180 40

Target 13. Control of analogues of substances under international control 181-187 42

Target 14. Identification of illicit narcotic plant cultivation 188-198 43

Target 15. Elimination of illicit plantings 199-209 45

Target 16. Redevelopment of areas formerly under illicit drug crop cultivation 210-222 48

III. SUPPRESSION OF ILLICIT TRAFFICKING 223-332 51

Introduction 223-230 51

Target 17. Disruption of major trafficking networks.... 231-248 52

Target 18. Promoting use of the technique of controlled delivery 249-252 55

Target 19. Facilitation of extradition 253-256 56

Target 20. Mutual judicial and legal assistance 257-265 57

Target 21. Admissibility in evidence of samples of bulk seizures of drugs 266-270 59

Target 22. Adequacy with a view to improved efficacy of penal provisions 271-277 60

Target 23. Forfeiture of the instruments and proceeds of illicit drug trafficking.................... 278-288 62

Target 24. Tightening of controls of movement through official points of entry 289-305 64

Target 25. Strengthening of external border controls and of mutual assistance machinery within economic unions of sovereign States 306-307 67

Target 26. Surveillance of land, water and air approaches to the frontier 308-320 67

Target 27. Controls over the use of the international mails for drug trafficking 321-325 69

Target 28. Controls over ships on the high seas and aircraft in international airspace 326-332 71

IV. TREATMENT AND REHABILITATION.............. 333-427 73

Introduction 333-337 73

Target 29. Towards a policy of treatment 338-348 74

Target 30. Inventory of available modalities and techniques of treatment and rehabilitation 349-361 76

Target 31. Selection of appropriate treatment programmes 362-378 78

		Paragraphs	*Page*

Target 32. Training for personnel working with drug addicts 379-388   80

Target 33. Reduction of the incidence of diseases and the number of infections transmitted through drug-using habits 389-395   82

Target 34. Care for drug-addicted offenders within the criminal justice and prison system 396-407   83

Target 35. Social reintegration of persons who have undergone programmes for treatment and rehabilitation 408-427   85

Index 89

A. Keywords of the Comprehensive Muldisciplinary Outline of Future Activities in Drug Abuse Control............................ 89

B. List of organizations 99

EXPLANATORY NOTES

The following abbreviations are used in this document:

CCC	Customs Co-operation Council
DND	Division of Narcotic Drugs
FAO	Food and Agriculture Organization of the United Nations
IATA	International Air Transport Association
ICAO	International Civil Aviation Organization
ICPO/Interpol	International Criminal Police Organization
ILO	International Labour Organisation
IMO	International Maritime Organization
INCB	International Narcotics Control Board
UNEP	United Nations Environment Programme
UNESCO	United Nations Educational, Scientific and Cultural Organization
UNFDAC or Fund	United Nations Fund for Drug Abuse Control
UPU	Universal Postal Union
WHO	World Health Organization
WTO	World Tourism Organization

For the sake of convenience and brevity, the word "drug" is used in this document to denote generally (unless the context obviously demands a different meaning):

(a) Any of the substances, whether natural or synthetic, included in Schedules I and II of the Single Convention on Narcotic Drugs, 1961, and that Convention as amended by the 1972 Protocol;[a]

(b) Any substance, natural or synthetic, or any natural material included in Schedules I, II, III and IV of the 1971 Convention on Psychotropic Substances.[b]

The expressions "drug abuse", "drug trafficking" and like terms should be construed accordingly.

The two Conventions are occasionally referred to in the text as "the 1961 Convention" and "the 1971 Convention".

---

[a]United Nations, *Treaty Series*, vol. 976, No. 14152, p.106.
[b]*Ibid.*, vol. 1019, No. 14956, p.176.

PART ONE

Declaration of the International Conference on Drug Abuse and Illicit Trafficking

We, the States participating in the International Conference on Drug Abuse and Illicit Trafficking,

Believing in human dignity and the legitimate aspirations of human-kind for a decent life with moral, humanitarian and spiritual values in a healthy, safe environment,

Concerned at the human suffering, loss of life, social disruption, especially the effect on youth who are the wealth of nations, brought about by drug abuse world-wide,

Aware of its effects on States' economic, social, political and cultural structures, and its threat to their sovereignty and security,

— Commit ourselves to vigorous international actions against drug abuse and illicit trafficking as an important goal of our policies;

— Express our determination to strengthen action and co-operation at the national, regional and international levels towards the goal of an international society free of drug abuse;

— Strive for the universal accession to the 1961 Single Convention on Narcotic Drugs or this Convention as amended by the 1972 Protocol and to the 1971 Convention on Psychotropic Substances and their strict implementation as well as the completion and adoption of the draft Convention against Illicit Trafficking in Narcotic Drugs and Psychotropic Substances, at the earliest possible date;

Agree on the following:

1. We express our determination to pursue the goals we have set for ourselves at various levels of government towards combating this scourge and to adopt urgent measures to strengthen international co-operation through a balanced, comprehensive and multidisciplinary approach. In this regard, we emphasize the pivotal role of Governments in developing appropriate national strategies within which such measures could be implemented.

2. In evolving effective action against drug abuse, illicit production and trafficking, we emphasize the need for the international community to adopt measures to treat all aspects and causes of the problem. To be effective, these measures must take into consideration the relevant social, economic and cultural factors and should be conducted in the context of States' policies in

1

this regard. We recognize the collective responsibility of the States to provide appropriate resources for the elimination of illicit production, trafficking and drug abuse.

3. We affirm the importance of and the need for wider adherence to the 1961 Single Convention on Narcotic Drugs or this Convention as amended by the 1972 Protocol and to the 1971 Convention on Psychotropic Substances. We call for the urgent but careful preparation and finalization, taking into account the various aspects of illicit trafficking, of the draft Convention Against Illicit Trafficking in Narcotic Drugs and Psychotropic Substances to ensure its entry into force at the earliest possible date and to complement existing international instruments.

4. We recognize the important role of the United Nations system in the efforts to combat drug abuse and illicit trafficking, and in particular the role of the Secretary-General of the United Nations in facilitating co-ordination and interaction among Member States and within the United Nations system. We attach importance to the role of the United Nations Commission on Narcotic Drugs as the policy-making body of the United Nations on drug control matters. We commend the positive action carried out by the Division of Narcotic Drugs, the International Narcotics Control Board and the United Nations Fund for Drug Abuse Control, and we urge strong national and international support for the Fund so as to enable it to fulfil its mandate.

5. We recognize the constant, determined efforts of Governments at the national, regional and international levels to counter the escalating incidence of drug abuse and illicit trafficking and the growing link between drug trafficking and other forms of international organized criminal activities.

6. We also recognize and welcome the significant role played by non-governmental organizations in the drive against drug abuse, and urge that further initiatives be encouraged to strengthen the efforts made at the national as well as international levels.

7. We welcome the compilation of the Comprehensive Multidisciplinary Outline of Future Activities in Drug Abuse Control as a compendium of possibilities for future action by all concerned.

8. Recognizing the magnitude and extent of the world-wide drug problem, we agree to intensify efforts against drug abuse and illicit trafficking. As an expression of our commitment, we also agree to promote inter-regional and international co-operation in:

(a) Prevention and reduction of demand;

(b) Control of supply;

(c) Suppression of illicit trafficking; and

(d) Treatment and rehabilitation.

For this purpose, we consider that the following, inter alia, should guide the development of our actions:

(a) Prevention and reduction of demand:
  (i) Develop methodologies and institute systems for assessing prevalence and trends of drug abuse on a comparable basis;

2

      (ii) Develop and implement the necessary measures to reduce drastically illicit demand through adequate techniques and programmes.

(b) Control of supply:

      (i) Encourage contributions from international financial institutions and Governments, where possible, for the implementation of programmes and projects for integrated rural development activities, including crop eradication/substitution schemes, and continue scientific research in related areas;

      (ii) Develop and implement the necessary procedures to eliminate the illicit supply of specific precursors and other materials necessary for the manufacture of narcotic drugs and psychotropic substances, and to prevent the diversion of pharmaceuticals to the illicit drug market.

(c) Suppression of illicit trafficking:

      (i) Develop bilateral and other instruments or arrangements for mutual legal assistance which might include among other things, if appropriate, extradition and tracing, freezing and forfeiture of assets, and for enhancing international legal or law enforcement co-operation in this field;

      (ii) Improve dissemination of information to national and international law enforcement bodies, especially concerning profiles and methods of operation of drug trafficking organizations, and further develop international, financial, technical and operational co-operation in investigation and training for officers and prosecutors.

(d) Treatment and rehabilitation:

      (i) Develop, promote and evaluate effective treatment and rehabilitation techniques;

      (ii) Provide health professionals and primary health care workers with information and training concerning appropriate medical use of narcotic drugs and psychotropic substances.

9. We affirm our determination to continue our efforts and request the Secretary-General of the United Nations to keep under constant review the activities referred to in this Declaration and in the Comprehensive Multidisciplinary Outline. We request the Secretary-General of the United Nations to propose in the context of the United Nations programme and budget and within available resources how the priority attached to the field of drug abuse control can best be carried out. The Commission on Narcotic Drugs should examine the most suitable modalities for following up these activities, as appropriate, at the international level.

PART TWO

Comprehensive Multidisciplinary Outline of Future Activities in Drug Abuse Control

INTRODUCTION

1.   The Comprehensive Multidisciplinary Outline of Future Activities in Drug Abuse Control is a repertory of recommendations addressed to Governments and to organizations setting forth practical measures which can contribute to the fight against drug abuse and to the suppression of illicit trafficking. At the national level, it is for each Government to determine which of the recommendations could be useful in its country in the light of economic and social conditions and to the extent consistent with national law. The Comprehensive Multidisciplinary Outline is not and was not designed to be a formal legal instrument; it does not create either rights or obligations of an international character. Its purpose will be achieved when the text is used as a handbook by national authorities and by interested organizations as a source of ideas to be selected and translated into action appropriate to local circumstances in the manner considered fit by these authorities and organizations. The text is accordingly drafted in non-mandatory style as a working guide, rather than as a package to be accepted in its entirety.

2.   The recommendations have been drafted in terms fully consistent with the principal international instruments concerned with drug abuse control; that is, the Single Convention on Narcotic Drugs, 1961, as amended by the 1972 Protocol Amending the Single Convention on Narcotic Drugs,[1] and the 1971 Convention on Psychotropic Substances of 1961.[2]

3.   In addition, with a view to safeguarding the principle of the sovereignty of the State and the primacy of the fundamental principles of the law and constitution of the State, many recommendations include a proviso concerning respect for these principles.

Background

4.   Throughout recorded history, substances to relieve suffering and to alter moods have been known and used in human societies. The ambivalence of these substances—they are indispensable for the relief of pain and suffering, but

---

[1]*United Nations Treaty Series*, vol. 976, No. 14152, p. 106

[2]*Ibid.*, vol. 1019, No. 14956, p. 176

addictive and destructive when misused or abused—led societies from earliest times to make rules restricting their use to religious or curative purposes and entrusting them only to priests or to healers and doctors.

5.   Since the mid-nineteenth century, drug abuse has been spreading in many countries as a result of a number of factors. The causes are many and vary in intensity; they include, in particular, the increased availability of products, the expansion of communications, socio-economic factors, migration and rapid urbanization, changes in attitudes and in the sense of values and the ruthless exploitation of fellow human beings by criminals.

6.   In order to deal with the increase in drug abuse, the community of nations has since the early twentieth century gradually evolved global control mechanisms intended to limit the availability of drugs for abuse, because it was quickly realized that no single country could succeed alone in preventing drug abuse and illicit trafficking. Between 1912 and 1972, no less than 12 multilateral drug control treaties were concluded. Under the auspices of the United Nations, the Single Convention on Narcotic Drugs, 1961, as amended by the 1972 Protocol, consolidated most of the earlier instruments, and the 1971 Convention on Psychotropic Substances created a system of international control for a number of previously uncontrolled psychoactive substances. During this period, the main effort was directed to the gradual devising and reinforcing of a network of administrative controls, having as its primary object the regulation of the supply and movement of drugs with a view to limiting their manufacture and import to the quantities required for legitimate medical and scientific purposes. Governments have also increasingly recognized the need to co-operate in the fight against the illicit production and manufacture of and traffic in drugs and accordingly to furnish to the international control organs, established first under the auspices of the League of Nations and then included in the United Nations system, periodic reports on their application of the international instruments and to submit to international supervision for their common benefit.

7.   As gaps in the international control system were progressively closed, it became more generally apparent that the mechanisms originally created for the introduction of international supply control were not in themselves a sufficient response to the current needs of the international community.

8.   Without prejudice to the importance of continuing administrative control of narcotic drugs and psychotropic substances and of international co-operation in the fight against the illicit traffic, counter-offensives of another dimension are now needed at the national and international levels to respond to the threat drug abuse poses not only to millions of persons but also to whole population groups and even to societies and economies in some countries. To take up the challenge it is necessary to intensify not only measures and programmes directed against the illicit production of and trafficking in drugs but also the activities undertaken to prevent the illicit demand for drugs and to further the treatment and eventual social reintegration of drug addicts.

9.   Many heads of State or Government have recently directed their personal attention to launching such counter-offensives, and the Secretary-General of the United Nations, addressing the Economic and Social Council on 24 May

1985, noted that the moment had arrived for the international community to expand its efforts in a global undertaking that would be more concerted and more comprehensive. He envisaged a truly world-wide effort to contain the plague of illicit drugs and thus proposed that a world conference be convened at the ministerial level in 1987 to deal with all aspects of drug abuse. Significant progress has already been achieved by the international community in building up defences against the production of addictive drugs and the illicit traffic in and abuse of those drugs. Building on this foundation of international co-operation developed over nearly 80 years, the international community is now concerting its efforts to expand the United Nations work in the field of drug abuse control and in the fight against illicit trafficking in drugs.

10. The political will on the part of the international community to take urgent, effective and concerted action to deal with the disturbing situation created by drug abuse and the illicit drug traffic was reflected in the decision of the General Assembly to convene the International Conference on Drug Abuse and Illicit Trafficking (hereinafter referred to as "the Conference") in 1987 (General Assembly resolution 40/122 of 13 December 1985). The Assembly gave the Conference an ambitious mandate, encompassing the full range of issues relevant to the fight against drug abuse, illicit trafficking and related criminal activities at the national, regional and international levels. It directed the Conference to adopt a "comprehensive multidisciplinary outline of future activities which focuses on concrete and substantive issues directly relevant to the problems of drug abuse and illicit trafficking" [paragraph 4(a)]. This mandate transcends the traditional concern with the control of the supply of and the illicit traffic in drugs and calls for a commitment by the Governments of all States to reinforce their individual efforts and to intensify and expand the scope of international co-operation into new areas.

Structure of the Comprehensive Multidisciplinary Outline of Future Activities in Drug Abuse Control

11. The Outline comprises four chapters, covering the main elements involved in the fight against drug abuse and illicit trafficking and the subjects included in the agenda of the Conference: the prevention and reduction of illicit demand; the control of supply; action against illicit trafficking; and treatment and rehabilitation.

12. Each chapter indicates specific targets, particularizing the objective to be attained and the action to be taken at the national level (by Governments, professional associations, academic institutions, non-governmental organiza-tions, communities, parents and individuals); at the regional level (by regional intergovernmental and non-governmental organizations and bodies); and at the international level (by international organizations, especially those of the United Nations system).

13. The catalogue of proposed actions is not exhaustive, nor does it follow any particular order of priority. At the national level, it would be for each State to determine its own order of priority among the targets, in the light of its own needs and resources. While all the targets are applicable to most countries, the modalities for the suggested courses of action are not necessarily applicable in

each instance. Any action should be considered within the socio-economic context of the country concerned and may need to be adapted to the particular cultural, social, political or legal setting in order to be successfully applied. In particular, due account being taken of the constitutional system, legislative and regulatory provisions and court practice may need to be adapted and revised in order to give full effect to national efforts.

General principles

14. The application of the recommendations contained in the Comprehensive Multidisciplinary Outline in the national setting implies the participation of many branches of the national governmental machinery—legislative organs; the authorities concerned with public health, education, social welfare, the judiciary, law enforcement and economic affairs; and all the many sectors in which the Government exercises responsibilities—and also institutions of higher learning, research and other academic bodies and private sector organizations. It is in this sense that the Outline is "multidisciplinary" in character.

15. If the contributions of these multifarious entities to a combined national effort are to be marshalled in support of the achievement of the objectives of the Outline, it then follows that machinery has to be established, where it does not yet exist, for co-ordinating the activities of these bodies, services, agencies and institutions. Indeed, the Outline, like the 1961 and 1971 Conventions, refers in numerous passages to national co-ordinating machinery. Accordingly, Governments which are determined to take effective action against drug abuse and illicit trafficking may find it advisable, and even indispensable, to set up a co-ordinating mechanism, in so far as they have not already done so, or to strengthen the existing machinery by establishing a nation-wide strategy. The national agency or authority designated to carry out this strategy could in turn be guided by certain general principles, which might include the following:

(*a*) A clear set of achievable objectives should be defined;

(*b*) Target groups should be clearly identified, priority being given to initiatives aimed at reducing drug abuse among young people;

(*c*) A balanced approach should be adopted for dealing with illicit demand, illicit supply and illicit trafficking;

(*d*) Programmes should be comprehensive and long-term;

(*e*) The development of the programmes and their implementation should be supported by research into the extent of drug abuse and its aetiology and consequences;

(*f*) The achievements of the programmes should be evaluated periodically;

(*g*) The work of all the agencies concerned at the national, regional (cantonal, provincial) and local levels should be part of a co-ordinated plan;

(*h*) The formulation of the national strategy should take into account in the first place the existing resources and, in the implementation of the strategy, a cost-effective approach should be adopted, with external support if necessary;

(*i*) The potential of community actions should be recognized and developed;

(*j*)   The national strategy could make the fullest possible use of the experience and attainments of other countries in fighting drug abuse and illicit trafficking, and the co-ordinating agency might offer to share its experiences with corresponding foreign authorities.

16.   The recommended measures set out in the CMO are intended to be applicable in the generality of situations where drug abuse or illicit trafficking, or both, have assumed dimensions that give rise to concern. National authorities are best equipped to judge what action is called for within the country for dealing with the evils of drug abuse and illicit trafficking. The recommended activities are designed to reinforce and not to replace those now undertaken in fulfilment of treaty obligations arising from the international conventions. At the same time, it cannot be too strongly emphasized that any State which is not yet a party to the two principal international instruments relating to drugs—the Single Convention, 1961 (as amended by the Protocol of 1972) and the 1971 Convention on Psychotropic Substances—should ratify or accede to these two Conventions as a matter of urgency, and so join the community of nations that is formally pledged to fight these evils by a common effort.* In addition, States parties to the Conventions should ensure that the provisions of these instruments are strictly applied. They are also urged to designate, in so far as they have not already done so, the special administrations or agencies referred to in articles 17 and 35 of the 1961 Convention and in articles 6 and 21 of the 1971 Convention.

17.   The restriction of the scope of the Comprehensive Multidisciplinary Outline to problems arising from the abuse of narcotic drugs and psychotropic substances should not be taken to imply that Governments should not consider taking action to combat the serious health consequences arising from the abuse of other substances, specifically alcohol and tobacco, since many of the drug demand reduction strategies in the Comprehensive Multidisciplinary Outline could be integrated into other government substance abuse prevention programmes.

---

*As of 1 June 1987, 115 States were parties to the 1961 Convention, 83 States were parties to the 1961 Convention as amended by the 1972 Protocol and 86 States were parties to the 1971 Convention.

Chapter I

PREVENTION AND REDUCTION OF THE ILLICIT DEMAND FOR NARCOTIC DRUGS AND PSYCHOTROPIC SUBSTANCES

Introduction

18.   Different authors and different Governments take different views as to the best way of fighting drug abuse and illicit trafficking and of dealing with their attendant phenomena. According to one school of thought, it is the sources of the illicit supply of drugs that should form the primary target of concerted and determined action, for—so it is argued—if the supply is halted or at least curtailed, addiction and trafficking would cease or at least diminish. Much of the national and international action taken so far has been aimed at the supply side of the drug economy, in the form of control of the legitimate production and trade (to prevent diversion into illicit channels), bans on cultivation of narcotic plants, and their eradication (physical uprooting or destroying of illicitly cultivated plants) etc. The philosophy underlying the two principal international instruments relating to narcotic and psychotropic substances—the 1961 and 1971 Conventions—is guided by the same considerations, in that they make provision for strict control, by licensing and other means, of the production, manufacture, internal and international trade, prescribing, storage etc. of the substances covered. In certain circumstances the cultivation of narcotic plants may be prohibited by the national authorities, and the two Conventions contain some provisions for penal sanctions to be enacted by States parties with respect to violations of the provisions of the Conventions which are treated as punishable offences.

19.   The inference to be drawn is that the manifest intention of the Conventions was to curb and prevent the uncontrolled flow of drugs and substances the non-medical consumption of which was considered dangerous to the health of the individual, to the social fabric and even in some cases to political stability and security.

20.   The other school of thought holds that efforts to deal with what has come to be regarded as a social scourge should concentrate on the illicit demand side, that is on the market. In the opinion of this school of thought, the more efficacious way of dealing with the criminal activities associated with drug abuse and illicit trafficking would be to lower the illicit demand for drugs.

21.   For the purpose of dealing with the totality of the problems posed by drug abuse and illicit trafficking, both the supply of and the demand for drugs

should be reduced and action should be taken to break the link between demand and supply, that is, the illicit traffic. It should also be recognized that an important deterrent to both the illicit demand and the illicit supply of drugs, as well as drug trafficking, is the existence of effective and enforced legal sanctions.

22. While it is not claimed that the restriction of the illicit demand is the panacea for the social sickness of drug abuse or for breaking the chain of criminal activities of illicit trafficking, various possible methods for reducing the illicit demand are suggested in chapter I. Nor should these suggestions be regarded in isolation or as contrasted with those put forward elsewhere in this Outline for curbing the illicit supply: Rather, they should be thought of as complementary to those other suggestions, for they all have ultimately the same objective of banishing an acknowledged evil and of rescuing human beings from a precarious situation.

23. To give attention to the fundamental causes of the problem of drug abuse, social, economic and cultural factors must be taken into account.

24. In some regions of the world, popular movements and voluntary organizations play a primary role in drug abuse prevention, education and awareness. The value of non-governmental organizations and government agencies working together on complex national and international problems is nowhere more apparent than in the comprehensive long-term effort to reduce illicit demand for narcotic drugs and psychotropic substances.

25. It will be noted that in chapter I considerable emphasis is laid on information, statistical data and exchanges of experience, for there is no doubt that there are large gaps in the knowledge about the extent of drug abuse and about methods for restraining it. To the extent that countries can learn from each other, and subject to due allowance for differences in resource endowment, social and cultural conditions and economic system, national authorities should be encouraged to ask for and communicate results of measures for reducing the illicit demand for drugs. For their part, the United Nations bodies concerned will wish to take into account, in projects or activities designed to alert the public to the risks of drug abuse and to diminish the illicit demand for drugs, the special need for protection of certain vulnerable population groups.

Target 1.   Assessment of the extent of drug misuse and abuse

The problem

26. Thanks to modern techniques of data gathering and processing, it is now possible in many countries to measure precisely the extent of drug use for medicinal purposes once a drug has been prescribed by doctors. Drug abuse, however, defies precise measurement, owing to its complexity and to its diffusion throughout a neighbourhood, city, region or nation.

27. A first point to consider is the meaning of the terms used: what effects of use are undesirable and which patterns are abusive? Under national law as well as under the international drug control treaties, a "narcotic drug" or a "psychotropic substance" is defined not in either the medical or scientific sense but rather in a legal sense as a substance included in a list determined by national or international law. At the same time, the use and possession of these specific substances are to be limited exclusively to medical and scientific purposes; misuse and abuse are, therefore, defined as illicit and are distinguished from the strictly medical use (i.e., medical administration or dispensing) by the legal status of the drug in question. Data contained in records of law enforcement agencies and of the judiciary will therefore only relate to unlawful use, whereas those from hospital emergency rooms will also include incidents caused by the use of substances that are not (or not yet) under control. The World Health Organization is developing a standardized nosology for drug abuse. The classification system will be valuable in clarifying the use of drug related terms, fostering communication and allowing for collaborative research.

28. Second, what is to be measured and by what methods? Surveys of illicit drug use can be unreliable, owing both to users' fears of exposure and to the fact that certain user groups cannot be reached by means of survey techniques. Surveys of illicit drug use can be unreliable for a number of reasons, including utilization of inappropriate methodology, under-reporting because of fear of exposure and the inability to sample certain user groups by survey techniques. In addition, owing to differences in statistical capability and approaches between countries, methods appropriate in one country may not be applicable in another. Research into the drug problem should be carried out by means of statistical studies and epidemiological surveys, in accordance with the circumstances.

Suggested courses of action

At the national level

29. The responsible authorities, in co-operation with all other ministries and services concerned or the national co-ordinating body where it exists, and with due regard for the national legislation safeguarding individual freedoms and rights to privacy could:

(*a*) Review current methodology for epidemiological studies of drug abuse and, where necessary, sponsor research leading to the development of more valid and reliable methodologies and instruments for assessing the extent of drug abuse;

(*b*) Review present methods of data collection by statistical, medical, legal and demographic services;

(*c*) Provide for the systematic collection of data on subpopulations of drug abusers from records of the police, registrars of deaths, courts (including coroners' courts), hospital emergency rooms, drug treatment centres, prisons, mental hospitals, psychiatric clinics, correctional institutions, social security and welfare organizations, schools and universities, the armed forces, employers, trade unions, as well as community agencies, institutions and associations;

(*d*) Establish training programmes for personnel involved in the collection and analysis of data;

(*e*) Establish central records for storing, analysing and evaluating data;

(*f*) Determine drug abuse patterns in special groups and environments, such as boarding schools, army bases, workplaces, prisons, hospitals;

(*g*) Determine, in respect of each type of drug of abuse:

   (i) The prevalence of active use (e.g., number of current users within a given period; say, the last year or the last month);

   (ii) Incidence of first use (e.g., number of new cases per year);

   (iii) Age at onset of use and the demography of users;

   (iv) Drug of abuse initially used and/or other drugs currently used;

   (v) The source of supply of currently abused drugs;

   (vi) Prevalence of use by sub-groups (e.g., males and females);

   (vii) Extent of use of particular drugs which cause diseases or affect special health conditions (e.g., pregnancy);

(*h*) Establish machinery for monitoring trends of abuse and evaluating the effectiveness of instruments, preventive policies, facilitate training, and the planning of prevention strategies;

(*i*) Test periodically the validity of the methodology used.

30. A country lacking a system for estimating the extent of drug abuse could develop such a system by stages, possibly with the assistance of WHO or any other international organization.

31. The appropriate authorities could undertake or sponsor studies to determine the frequency or gravity of drug addiction (or addiction to particular drugs) in specific population groups and the connection (if any) that exists between drug addiction and a variety of social, economic and cultural factors. These studies could include both particular and general factors related to the individual, the family, and society. It is recommended that the results of the studies be brought to the attention of the agency or authority responsible for the social services that need to be mobilized in order to lessen the illicit demand for drugs.

32. Universities, research institutes and other academic institutions should conduct studies to determine the implications of present patterns of drug abuse in terms of predicted demographic developments.

33. If the appropriate authority has reason to suspect, in the light of statistical or other data, that a change has taken place or is about to take place in the pattern of consumption of addictive drugs (e.g. a shift towards a newly "fashionable" drug among drug users, or a marked rise in illicit demand in a particular locality), it should instruct the appropriate agencies to investigate the circumstances and possible causes of the suspected phenomenon promptly and to report back with recommendations for dealing with the situation. In countries where an "early warning" system of this nature does not already exist, the authority concerned may consider the establishment of such machinery if in its opinion the situation warrants it.

At the regional and international levels

34. Regional organizations should make comparative studies of drug abuse patterns in countries in the region and inquire into reasons for variations in drug abuse (patterns, methods etc.).

35. Formal agreements should be established for international collaboration, using comparable methodology and instrumentation, so that resulting data can provide measures of international drug abuse patterns. Field testing of the common methodology and instrumentation is essential.

36. National focal points of States in the region concerned might share information on drug abuse and on methodologies for determining its incidence and prevalence, as well as exchanging experiences.

37. Ongoing information collection, analysis and dissemination activities within the United Nations system, including in particular the regional commissions, should include data on the full range of drug abuse issues in their areas of responsibility in order to permit an integrated approach to activities touching on drug abuse (e.g. activities concerning social development policy and planning, integrated rural development, popular participation, women and youth). Country focal points could be invited to collaborate closely with the regional commissions in this effort.

38. Regional organizations should establish training programmes for personnel engaged or about to be engaged in epidemiological surveys; expert knowledge available in the region should be used in the first instance for this purpose.

39. The United Nations Secretariat (Division of Narcotic Drugs), in association with WHO and regional and international organizations as well as non-governmental organizations, should disseminate information on the experiences of States in developing an appropriate methodology for assessing drug abuse.

40. The Division of Narcotic Drugs, in co-operation with WHO, should prepare and publish handbooks suggesting methodologies for collecting and analysing data on drug abuse.

41. The United Nations Fund for Drug Abuse Control (UNFDAC), in co-operation with WHO and other international organizations, should include among its priorities providing assistance to States, at their request, in support of their own efforts to establish standardized systems of case registration as well as to carry out surveys of the causes, extent and patterns of drug abuse and assistance in training specialized personnel to collect, analyse and evaluate data.

42. Technical assistance in the planning and carrying out of epidemiological surveys should be provided to States by international organizations, such as WHO, and by countries with the necessary expertise.

Target 2. Organization of comprehensive systems for the collection and evaluation of data

The problem

43.   Crude indicators of future trends in drug use and abuse are available from many sources, including the records of medical practitioners, hospitals, social insurance agencies, school administrators, police, customs authorities and courts. Medical associations world-wide should also be urged to co-operate in assembling this information in collaboration with WHO. This information should be taken into account, subject to respect for confidentiality, in the formulation of national policies intended to prevent abuse and reduce demand for the drugs in question.

44.   To be useful to policy-makers, this information, which in general exists only in the records of the agency or person concerned, needs to be collected, collated and analysed, preferably by a system or machinery designed for this specific purpose, with particular emphasis on the consistency and comparability of national and regional data.

Suggested courses of action

At the national level

45.   The appropriate national authority could, as a beginning, appoint a working group to devise simple, easy-to-use, reliable standardized instruments that may:

   (*a*)   Facilitate the gathering of common information about drug abuse from agencies concerned with different aspects of the abuse;

   (*b*)   Be used by all entities concerned for collecting basic descriptive data;

   (*c*)   Be used nationally as a foundation for epidemiological surveys.

46.   At the local and national levels, a simple framework could be created for the collation of data sheets. The data could be made freely available, without disclosure of names or personal particulars to agencies and individuals involved in research and/or planning. Mechanisms could be established for sharing the data among appropriate policy-makers and drug abuse professionals. Sharing encourages common data collection techniques and makes it possible to give early warning of new drug use patterns.

47.   Field trials of the reliability and validity of any instruments should be conducted and independently analysed by appropriate researchers.

48.   In addition to sponsoring measures and activities designed to reduce the illicit demand for drugs, the ministry concerned (health, education, social welfare, as the case may be) might inquire into the multiple possible causes of drug abuse and, as appropriate, recommend action for eliminating the causes, or at least the most serious of them. The inquiries might, as appropriate, take the form of surveys of the social and family circumstances of drug addicts or groups of addicts or persons at risk to drug abuse, their housing, employment,

level of education and any other characteristic that may appear as a contributory cause of drug abuse. Research should be conducted whenever possible to evaluate the effectiveness of the programmes and techniques utilized by States to reduce drug abuse.

49. In view of the constant evolution of the pharmaceutical industry, of continuing intensive research into the properties of newly discovered drugs and their effects on the human organism and of the risk of abuse, the appropriate authority could make regulations or issue orders (in so far as these do not already exist) directing local health authorities, medical practitioners, pharmacists, directors of educational establishments and research institutes to report to it promptly any case that has come to their notice of persons showing symptoms of incipient addiction to a newly or recently discovered drug or substance or to a pharmaceutical product, previously considered innocuous, which is found to possess narcotic or hallucinogenic properties. The authority concerned might consider whether the product or substance in question should be placed under control or, as the case may be, under stricter control.

At the regional and international levels

50. Standardized instruments developed by appropriate national authorities should be field-tested and, if found useful, made available for the collection of comparable data. National authorities should determine what kinds of data are needed to address key issues, e.g. incidence, prevalence, risk factors and aetiology. Governments might collaborate with each other and with appropriate international organizations, e.g. WHO and the Division of Narcotic Drugs, in an effort to identify common risk factors and establish prospective studies to determine if these factors are predictive.

51. Provisional data sheets for pilot studies should be initially drawn up in a small number of States; if found useful, such studies might be carried out in a larger number of countries.

52. Technical assistance might be made available for the purpose of standardized record keeping, making due allowance for the social and cultural setting in which instruments will be used.

53. The committees established in New York and at Vienna by international non-governmental organizations in consultative status with the Economic and Social Council that have an interest in the control of drug abuse and illicit traffic are invited to act as a clearing-house of relevant information for dissemination to national non-governmental organizations concerned with drug abuse acting as focal points.

54. In regions where the dimensions of illicit drug trafficking and drug abuse are very imperfectly known and where the laws and the practices of the agencies concerned with the suppression of these illegal activities vary greatly from country to country, a unit at the headquarters of the regional commission might co-operate with existing specialized bodies of the United Nations system and other international organizations in identifying the needs of their member countries for strengthening drug control. Where there is a need for improved

law enforcement to combat illicit drug trafficking, such a unit could usefully co-operate with the International Criminal Police Organization (ICPO/Interpol) and the Customs Co-operation Council (CCC) in their joint regional programme involving, *inter alia*, the holding of regular working meetings of senior police and customs officials, with a view to increasing co-operation and exchange of information between police and customs authorities, both nationally and internationally. If a regional commission originates regional projects for this purpose, consideration might be given to the granting of support for such projects from sources within the United Nations system.

55.   The Governments of countries in a region in which the illicit use of and traffic in drugs give rise to common concern, and in which common action is desirable at the regional level for the purpose of warding off drug abuse and illicit trafficking in these countries or in some of them, may wish to consider the establishment of a regional centre for scientific research and education that would contribute to the fight against drug abuse and illicit traffic (as envisaged in article 38 *bis* of the 1961 Convention).

Target 3.   Prevention through education

The problem

56.   Comprehensive and effective education programmes are a necessary part of measures for counteracting drug abuse world-wide. In many countries drug abuse has already spread to the various age and population groups. It is essential that all individuals in the formal and general education system, as well as their families, should be enlightened about the risks of drug abuse.

57.   Prevention through education should be considered as a continuous process and a lengthy exacting action, the objective of which is to seek and improve understanding of the long-term and immediate causes of recourse to drugs, to help young people and adults to find solutions to their difficulties and to lead their lives without resorting to drugs.

58.   Curricula and programmes for enhancing the community's awareness, developed where appropriate as part of an agreed national strategy, should be so constructed as to strengthen the population's motivation to avoid drug abuse. Indications are that the impact of preventive education is greatest when it:

  (*a*)   takes place in its appropriate social, economic and cultural setting;

  (*b*)   is integrated into the overall framework of academic, social and cultural learning;

  (*c*)   promotes a healthy drug-free life-style as a primary goal, as opposed to placing emphasis on abstinence from drugs and on the negative effects of drug abuse;

  (*d*)   reaches individuals before they are exposed to the drug sub-culture and other influences that contribute to initial drug use;

  (*e*)   does not involve elements that evoke curiosity or the desire to experiment with narcotic drugs (detailed "positive" descriptions of euphoria etc.), but clearly indicates the negative, harmful consequences of drug abuse and emphasizes the positive effects of alternative activities and a life-style free from narcotic drugs and psychotropic substances; and

(f)   does not contain details which might make access to illicit drugs easy, such as detailed descriptions of methods and routes of illicit traffic in narcotic drugs, places of origin of illicit production, non-medical uses of narcotic drugs etc.

59.   Care should be taken that preventive education in school and out-of-school does not become yet another addition to curricula and that additional costs are avoided. Where advisable, attention should be paid to integrating progressively into school curricula and out-of-school activities an element concerning the prevention of drug abuse within the framework of activities for the improvement of the quality of life and which would be attached to existing disciplines and curricula. Continuity and the development of the prevention of drug abuse will thus be assured, without extending curricula which are already overloaded and without involving additional costs for the educational system.

Suggested courses of action

At the national level

60.   The appropriate authority could establish a multidisciplinary unit in which teaching personnel who have received training in the subject of prevention must be represented. The unit would perform such functions as:

(a)   Prescribing or recommending for all levels of educational institutions the development of drug abuse prevention curricula and instructional materials, taking into account cultural values and traditions and emphasizing the benefits of a healthy drug-free life-style;

(b)   Preparing training and educational materials for the unemployed and undereducated, especially the young people, to assist them in developing vocational and self-employment skills;

(c)   Within the school system, teacher education and motivation are essential to ensure the effective education of children regarding drugs and healthy life-styles. Therefore, it is essential to prepare training materials and to conduct training programmes for teachers and counsellors that will enable them to instruct their students in the advantages of a drug-free life. The teachers themselves must play an important role in the preparation of these training materials and programmes. This prevention instruction must be provided by the teachers themselves and should in no case become a separate course; on the contrary, it should be made an integral part of as many courses as possible;

(d)   Preparing basic information publications on drug abuse and the different models of prevention, and acting as a focal point for the collection, collation and dissemination of information about drug abuse and the different models of prevention. Particular attention should be given to ensuring that preventive instruction at school is not instituted as an isolated, one-time measure, but rather that it is designed as a long-term programme accompanied by preventive measures involving students, parents, workers, the clergy, doctors and pharmacists. Only a comprehensive approach at the regional and local levels will have a chance of success;

(*e*) Undertaking periodic reviews of the curricula characteristics and publicity material in question to determine their effectiveness, and recommending adjustments as necessary that promote, on behalf of the authority responsible for education, training sessions for interested members of the teaching staff.

(*f*) Preparing programmes and information relative to promoting drug-free sport, cultural and leisure time facilities and activities.

61. The appropriate authorities could give priority to the training of educational personnel for both school and out-of-school activities (e.g. teachers, educators, monitors, counsellors, inspectors, headmasters). At the level of pre-service training, all educational personnel should be familiarized with problems of drug abuse and prevention techniques. In-service courses should be organized in specialized areas for certain categories of personnel.

62. The authorities responsible for public education might formulate a school policy aimed at preventing drug abuse, its implementation to be monitored by school administrators, in consultation, as appropriate, with teachers, students and parents. In particular, student leaders should be encouraged to develop attitudes and activities in their schools and communities aimed at preventing drug abuse. Seminars and training courses should be established to help parents recognize the symptoms of drug abuse at the early stages and to enable them to educate their children to recognize the damaging physical and mental effects of drug abuse.

63. School boards and authorities responsible for private and denominational schools should similarly formulate school policies aimed at preventing drug abuse, consonant with their curricula, and develop training and instructional material for classroom and related community use.

64. Interested members of the training staff and school and guidance counsellors should be given training to advise students and parents about the dangers of drug abuse.

65. An important milieu for the education of the young is the family. Programmes should be developed to educate parents about the harmful effects of drug use and about methods to develop the competence skills of their own children.

66. The authority responsible at the national or local level, in conjunction with other appropriate authorities, might issue instructions or recommendations or provide consultation and advice to institutions responsible for training persons for a profession in which they will be concerned with the prevention or treatment of drug abuse (social workers, police, medical practitioners, paramedical personnel, health teachers) to include in their curricula or programmes of study a course specially designed to enable such persons to recognize and deal with cases of drug abuse.

67. In view of the vulnerability of young persons to the temptations offered by certain narcotic and psychotropic substances and to the solicitations of

"drug pushers", the appropriate authority may consider establishing publicity and educational programmes to alert young people and society in general, particularly in urban areas, to the dangers with which the consumption of dangerous, habit-forming and dependence-producing substances is fraught: disruption of family and social life, health risks, impairment of intellectual capability, perversion of moral values and antisocial and criminal behaviour.

68. The national co-ordinating agency, where it exists, or the appropriate authority could consider favourably the idea of establishing a small body composed of experts, representatives of agencies and other persons familiar, through their research or professional activity, with the situation regarding drug abuse in the country (e.g. teachers, social workers, members of the police force, representatives of national non-governmental organizations and others) who would be given the mandate to design a programme (where it does not already exist) intended specifically to reduce and ultimately prevent the illicit demand for drugs in a particular population group such as, and especially, youth. The programme would make provision for the training of specialized personnel to be deployed at the national and local level for the purpose of implementing demand-reducing schemes. Prevention programmes should be designed not only in the light of the dangers of drug consumption but on the basis of educational messages inculcating an active sense of responsibility with respect to the quality of life.

At the regional and international levels

69. Regional bodies should consider establishing regional training, resource and information centres for individuals involved in designing curricula, in order to evaluate and develop teaching techniques consonant with the cultural patterns of the region and to disseminate these techniques by means of regional courses and exchange of personnel.

70. The United Nations Educational, Scientific and Cultural Organization (UNESCO) and other international and non-governmental organizations might, at the regional level, encourage the creation of co-operative networks among institutions, programmes and projects dealing especially with preventive action and, at the request of Member States, provide data on strategies, methods and experience in prevention through education, facilitate and encourage the exchange of educational personnel and participate in the identification and development of programmes aiming at the prevention of drug abuse. Specific initiatives should be encouraged to promote exchanges of experience between countries having similar problems.

71. In cases where projects with an educational content are envisaged for the purpose of preventing and reducing the illicit demand for drugs, the Government or regional or international bodies or non-governmental organizations sponsoring or initiating the projects may, if they lack funds, apply for support to the United Nations Fund for Drug Abuse Control which should give priority to such projects.

72. Programmes and projects of United Nations organizations, especially the regional commissions, dealing with vulnerable population groups should

include information about the scope and nature of drug abuse problems, their causes, and preventive and remedial actions as they relate to these groups.

73.   Where large groups of refugees are receiving care (including health and educational care) from an intergovernmental organization and where cases of drug abuse have been noted among them, the organization concerned should investigate such cases and ascertain their frequency and gravity and, in the light of the information, issue warnings of the dangers of drug abuse (especially among the young) within the refugee population and, if possible, undertake an educational, cultural and therapeutic programme for refugee groups at risk. Any relevant activity should be carried out in co-operation and in accord with the State of asylum.

Target 4.   Prevention of drug abuse in the workplace

The problem

74.   The multiple and harmful consequences associated with drug abuse in the workplace and in occupational activities include deterioration of productivity and performance, defective quality of products, loss of qualified employees, accidents, loss of income and professional disqualification, all of which are costly to the individual, the employer, and the community.

75.   Where alcohol abuse prevention programmes exist, consideration should be given to applying the experience gained in these programmes to the prevention and reduction of the abuse of drugs in the workplace.

76.   Drug abuse by individuals in a wide range of sensitive occupations can result in disaster. Measures for dealing with drug abuse in the workplace and in occupational activities must have a significant prevention component.

Suggested courses of action

   At the national level

77.   With a view to preventing or reducing drug abuse in the workplace, the authority concerned could:

   (*a*)   Publicize information in the workplace warning of the risks of drug abuse;

   (*b*)   Set up national training workshops for supervisors, programme developers and others.

78.   The appropriate authority, after consulting the parties concerned, might issue guidelines drawing the attention of employers and workers and of their organizations to the resources, in the form of publicity material, information through the media etc., that can be made available to them in connection with programmes for preventing or reducing drug abuse in the workplace, and for treating and rehabilitating drug addicts.

79. Special emphasis should be placed on the urgent need to prevent abuse of drugs by those persons who are often regarded as role models. Professional and occupational associations should accordingly develop drug abuse prevention programmes for their members.

80. Employers' and workers' organizations should develop joint action programmes for their memberships with a view to discouraging drug abuse.

81. Medical authorities and medical laboratories should design reliable testing methods for the purpose of determining the presence of drugs in the human organism, identifying drug users and ensuring the safety of the public.

At the regional and international levels

82. The Governments of countries in a region could, through the ministries concerned or through regional bodies or non-governmental organizations, identify regional resources for training and programme development. They should organize regional seminars, as necessary, for the exchange of experiences and dissemination of relevant information. The International Labour Organisation (ILO) might be invited to initiate and participate actively in the intensification of the exchange of experiences at the regional and international levels.

83. The ILO should be invited, in co-operation with UNESCO, to co-ordinate international efforts to prevent and reduce drug abuse in the workplace, for example by distributing multimedia resource kits for the promotion and implementation of programmes to control, prevent and treat drug abuse in the workplace and to rehabilitate former drug abusers in employment; it might in addition monitor the use of these kits and the results thereof.

84. The Division of Narcotic Drugs, in collaboration with WHO and ILO, should promote and harmonize national efforts by developing internationally acceptable guidelines, criteria and methodologies for national testing programmes; a central source of reference standards of major drug metabolites should be established to serve national laboratories.

Target 5. Prevention programmes by civic, community and special interest groups and law enforcement agencies

The problem

85. The support and involvement of community organizations, as well as law enforcement, health, social and educational agencies involved in the prevention of drug abuse, are indispensable in counteracting the harmful factors that foster drug abuse. Community organizations and health and social agencies are well situated to detect drug abuse and its consequences and to identify groups at risk. Moreover, these organizations and law enforcement agencies are aware of the needs, resources and goals of their members.

86. Hence, the local community and law enforcement agencies should not only adopt drug abuse prevention as part of their basic goals but should also be fully conversant with the objectives of national prevention programmes and should initiate or participate in the formulation and implementation of such programmes.

87. Most community activities are voluntary. Effective co-ordination is therefore required to ensure that community projects and activities for preventing drug abuse are consistent with the national plans for drug abuse prevention, and they should be periodically evaluated for efficacy. To the degree possible and when appropriate, representatives of the educational system should be involved in the co-ordination function.

Suggested courses of action

At the national level

88. All civic groups, associations and clubs, especially those directly concerned with youth and other groups at risk, should prepare and disseminate to their members information drawing attention to the dangers of drug abuse. Voluntary organizations might, for example, be asked to provide package programmes of counselling and guidance, preventive education, drug abuse awareness, referral, detoxification, aftercare and rehabilitation. To the degree possible these activities should be co-ordinated to ensure consistency with national policy and, where appropriate, with international recommendations for the prevention of drug abuse.

89. National voluntary agencies, religious groups, political parties, civic organizations, parent-teacher associations, and other community-wide associations should make a point of publicizing the advantages of a drug-free lifestyle and educating the public about the dangers of drug abuse. Professional associations (e.g. pharmaceutical, medical, teaching, social workers) should promote the voluntary participation of their members in prevention programmes both within their communities and among their members.

90. For the purpose of taking action to prevent the illicit demand for drugs it is essential to impress upon the public the value of good health as a component in ensuring the quality of life. Community activities should emphasize the importance of positive cultural values and a sound social basis enhancing the quality of life without drug abuse.

91. Initiatives at the national, regional and local levels should strive for a co-ordination of actions among the agencies responsible for health, justice, education and other appropriate agencies. This collaborative effort among agencies and groups should promote a comprehensive approach to the drug problem. Channels of communication should accordingly be established, in accordance with relevant national legislation, by community organizations with representative target groups in order to achieve a better understanding of the effects of drug abuse (e.g. hotlines, peer group counselling).

92. The ministry concerned (justice, interior, education, finance, health, religious or social affairs, as the case may be) might consider, if appropriate in the societal and cultural setting, sponsoring and, if necessary or desirable, supporting with financial or other resources the participation of representatives of certain law enforcement agencies in activities aimed at informing the public or specific sectors of the public about what is being done and could be done to prevent drug abuse. Representatives of the agencies in question (police, customs service, judiciary) might give talks describing their operations against drug abuse, suggesting how the community, the family and educational establishments should contribute to the campaign against drug abuse and indicating the willingness of the agencies to co-operate in local initiatives to enlighten the population about the dangers of drug abuse. Similarly, the national authorities responsible for monitoring the manufacture and distribution of pharmaceutical products, in association with the representative organization of pharmaceutical manufacturers, might participate in such campaigns. These campaigns could include the concept that prescription drugs should be taken only when, and in the manner, prescribed.

At the regional and international levels

93. Regional meetings of various civic groups should be periodically convened to exchange information on action that has improved community activities for the prevention of drug abuse.

94. Regional organizations should encourage increased participation of non-governmental organizations and their own communities in their efforts to combat drug abuse and illicit trafficking. The activities of the non-governmental organizations in the fight against drug abuse should be co-ordinated, as appropriate, in close co-operation with national Governments, other co-ordinating bodies, and relevant agencies in their regions.

95. The agencies concerned, communities and educational systems, including law enforcement agencies of countries in the same region, should be encouraged to co-ordinate their regional activities for the purpose of conducting a campaign against drug abuse at the regional or international levels, for example by participating in regional meetings dealing with drug abuse and its prevention or undertaking other joint efforts to curb drug abuse and illicit trafficking. Similarly, these agencies should be encouraged to enter into or broaden contacts with counterparts in countries outside the region, with a view to planning world-wide activities to counter drug abuse. International and intergovernmental organizations such as the Inter-Parliamentary Union, ICPO/Interpol and CCC might have a useful role to play in arranging such contacts.

96. International non-governmental organizations should:

(a) Be encouraged to collate and disseminate information on national and regional activities of their constituent organizations, keeping in mind the need to foster more communication between governmental and non-governmental organizations;

(b) Facilitate discourse between their constituent national organizations and other non-governmental organizations concerned on community action that has had some success;

(c) Help their constituent organizations to formulate programmes that would give effect to recommendations by international bodies concerning the prevention of drug abuse;

(d) At their own request, be given the support of the United Nations and the specialized agencies concerned in carrying out programmes for the prevention of drug abuse;

(e) Work out ways in which to undertake co-operative efforts with the United Nations and with Governments.

Target 6. Leisure-time activities in the service of the continuing campaign against drug abuse

The problem

97. It is in the community's interest to ensure that leisure time is used constructively. A wide range of activities, such as community service and sporting and cultural activities, should provide alternatives to drug abuse for the various social groups, particularly for the young, the elderly and the disabled. Studies have demonstrated that substantial benefits can be realized for both groups by fostering contact between the elderly and youth. Moreover, leisure-time activities can exert a positive effect on individuals, as they improve social adaptation and tend to develop skills, talent and a sense of responsibility.

98. If alternative activities are to be in any way successful, target groups must be motivated and encouraged to participate in the design, initiation and running of leisure-time activities of interest to them. This is particularly important in areas of high unemployment and youth unemployment, and for risk groups living in isolation, which are especially vulnerable to the misuse of prescription drugs.

99. While community groups should initiate and design leisure-time activities, government support in the provision of resources, facilities and materials is often necessary. Governmental support for alternatives to drug abuse can serve as an important counterbalance to certain types of commercial entertainment where drug abuse is idealized or glorified. At the same time, such support tends to ensure a reciprocal flow of information.

Suggested courses of action

At the national level

100. Within the resources available, local government authorities should provide facilities, materials and funding to promote drug-free leisure-time activities. Such leisure-time activities, in the service of drug abuse prevention, should reinforce cultural and familial values, enhance health, and encourage positive social behaviour.

101.   Community groups and government agencies concerned might review the existing range of leisure-time activities and develop programmes tending to promote wholesome and drug-free cultural and sporting activities. They could, in addition, make sure that those responsible for organizing cultural and sporting events, and the participants themselves, abstain from any action that might, explicitly or implicitly, give the public a misleading impression of the nature of drug abuse.

102.   The appropriate authority might develop guidelines and suggested courses of action for use by public and private travel agencies, operators of transport undertakings and other bodies concerned with passenger travel and tourism urging them to refrain from publishing or disseminating material advertising, overtly or surreptitiously, the easy availability of narcotic or psychotropic drugs in any particular country or area. The authority might also consider posting notices at official points of entry into the country, warning travellers of the penalties applicable in respect of illicit dealing in drugs.

At the regional and international levels

103.   Sporting and cultural organizations of countries in the region, in co-operation with the national authorities concerned, should promote and expand sporting and cultural exchanges, with an emphasis on drug-free events.

104.   Information on local drug laws should be included with information for travellers on tourist activities (available, for example, at international borders and in hotels and youth hostels).

Target 7.   Role of the media

The problem

105.   The mass media reach a vast audience every day. While the media's potential contribution to the campaign for preventing drug abuse is enormous, their publications and broadcasts can also be damaging and counterproductive. The use of inaccurate or misleading terminology regarding narcotic drugs and psychotropic substances and their properties, such as the artificial distinction between so-called "hard" and "soft" drugs, the advocacy of legalization of the non-medical use of drugs, the glamorizing of drug abuse in songs, movies and other commercial products, the emphasis given in reports of the street value of seizures to the enormous profits to be made from the illicit drug traffic, and the association of drug use with the names of successful or famous persons—all these can lead to false perceptions and can flaw the individual's powers of judgement.

106.   Poorly designed campaigns to prevent drug abuse may also have the opposite effect from that intended, by arousing curiosity and inducing, rather than preventing, undesirable behaviour. It is vital, therefore, that there should be continuous research and evaluation of action taken, programmes imple-

mented and the impact of messages transmitted by the media. In addition, care should be taken to ensure that the fundamental human rights of freedom of speech and of the press and of other forms of expression are respected.

Suggested courses of action

At the national level

107. The appropriate authority concerned with broadcasting, the film industry and other media, if it has not already done so, might consider drawing up guidelines in the form of codes of conduct to be observed voluntarily by the public and private enterprises concerned in portraying or representing any event or incident involving the abuse of drugs. In addition, it may wish to recommend the observance of any guidelines of like nature that have been approved in an international forum.

108. Health agencies and other organizations concerned should more actively seek the support of the media as responsible advocates of a drug-free life-style. This could be achieved by convening, on a regular basis, workshops, briefings, information sessions etc. for media personnel to increase their knowledge of drug abuse and their awareness of the efforts of governmental and non-governmental agencies to counteract the problem.

109. In addition, in so far as it has not already done so, the authority concerned might consider:

(a) Inviting or, as appropriate, instructing local and central agencies responsible for drug control to designate, in the particular territory or area, a person or group of persons to act as liaison with the media and to provide the media with information and advice about the risks of drug abuse;

(b) Encouraging programme planners to consult the media on the portrayal of drugs and drug abuse in the broadcasting of drama and news items, and to provide them with appropriate material so as to ensure that news items are presented in a factual manner which does not, intentionally or unintentionally, mislead the audience or glamorize drug abuse;

(c) Through its agencies, enrolling the media in co-operative efforts to reduce the illicit demand for drugs.

110. Media executives might be brought into partnership with government and the community and invited: (a) to assist in the formulation of programmes in support of preventive policies and efforts; (b) to provide factual and honest information on drug abuse; and (c) to formulate programmes that promote cultural values and a healthy life-style. To the extent possible, continuous co-operation between educational authorities and the media should be encouraged.

111. Governments and non-governmental organizations concerned might co-operate in selecting research relating, for example, to an understanding of patterns of drug consumption. Such research should be supported by advertisers and public relations and public opinion researchers.

112. All means of communication and, in particular, the mass media, whether in the public or in the private sector, might be invited to participate in a

concerted and long-term effort by nation-wide and local authorities and community groups to enhance the public image of a drug-free life, to disparage the drug-taking habit that has spread to certain classes of society, to induce all population groups to become health conscious and to realize the hazards associated with drug abuse, and to urge parents, teachers, community leaders and persons in public life to set an example by abstaining from drug abuse.

113. The appropriate authority could consider establishing channels of communication through which suggestions or recommendations might be addressed, informally and without implying any interference that might smack of censorship, to persons or bodies responsible for the management of radio or television broadcasting or other mass media. The media should voluntarily comply with requests by the authorities concerned with drug control to refrain from publicizing any news relating to ongoing investigations of drug-related offences.

114. In countries where several languages are spoken and understood, the appropriate authority, in conjunction with any other authorities concerned and with the co-operation of the media, could consider ensuring that warnings about the harm caused by drug abuse are broadcast, disseminated or prominently displayed on public premises and in schools, youth and sports clubs etc. in the various languages used in the country.

115. In countries with a high rate of illiteracy, the authority concerned could consider publicizing such warnings by audio, visual or graphic means, e.g. posters, photographs etc., or by sending representatives of the public health service to rural areas to spread the warning by word of mouth. Anti-drug education should be recommended for inclusion in literacy programmes. The authority may also wish to use the good offices of "grass-roots" organizations for this purpose.

116. In view of the vital importance of information in planning and carrying out a programme to restrain and reduce the illicit demand for controlled drugs, the appropriate authority could prepare television spots, notices, leaflets, pamphlets or other material seeking information from all sources (including those not in the health system) that may lead to improved, more accurate information on illicit demand and also contribute to the formulation by the media of programmes for curbing this demand.

117. Mothers and fathers may need to be alerted to the ways of preventing their children from becoming drug abusers and of weaning themselves from drug abuse if they have contracted the habit.

118. Drug abuse during pregnancy may lead to serious effects for the child. Special emphasis should therefore be placed on informing young women of the specific dangers of drug abuse during pregnancy.

At the regional and international levels

119. UNESCO, in co-operation with specialized non-governmental organizations, could facilitate exchanges of audio-visual material which could be used in

preventive action, contribute to the evaluation of information campaigns and implement international co-operative research on the impact of messages transmitted by the media.

120.   Periodic meetings of journalists and media executives from different countries might be organized by the professional organizations concerned to exchange views on the portrayal of drug abuse in the media.

121.   Regional and international bodies should be invited to offer training courses for journalists who report on drug issues to improve the accuracy of their reports and to avoid conveying false impressions to their readers and viewers.

122.   With a view to stimulating the production of audio and visual programmes on the prevention of drug abuse, the creation of an international prize or award to recompense the best amongst them should be envisaged.

Chapter II

CONTROL OF SUPPLY

Introduction

123. A most important achievement of the international community in controlling the supply of drugs has been the development of a system for the international control of narcotic drugs, which includes control of the cultivation, production, manufacture and use of and international trade in substances controlled under the Single Convention on Narcotic Drugs, 1961, and that Convention as amended by the 1972 Protocol. The object of the system is to achieve a world-wide equilibrium between demand for and supply of narcotic drugs for licit purposes and to prevent their diversion to illicit channels.

124. In view of the huge growth in the illicit demand for opiates in many countries in the past two decades, an illegal heroin "industry" has developed, involving illicit or uncontrolled opium poppy cultivation and the illegal production and distribution of opium, heroin and other opiates. A complicating factor is that opiates have a recognized medical value and that no adequate substitutes have as yet been approved for certain applications. Consequently, the international control system provides for restricted cultivation of limited amounts of the opium poppy carefully calculated to correspond to the estimated annual medical requirements of each State. With a view to strengthening the treaty provisions relating to the control of poppy straw, it has been suggested that the full range of measures of control applicable to opium should be extended to poppy straw. According to another view, however, the provisions of the amended 1961 Convention are adequate. The treaties also provide that licit cultivation of the opium poppy for commercial purposes other than the production of opium or for the production of poppy straw is also authorized, provided that all necessary measures are taken to ensure that no opium is produced from such poppies and that the manufacture of drugs from poppy straw is adequately controlled.

125. The eradication of illicitly cultivated opium poppy, coca bush and cannabis plants is a complex undertaking, because they are often grown in remote areas, or in areas beyond effective government control. Additional complications arise because in some developing countries these crops sometimes provide supplementary sources of livelihood for the rural population.

126. Cocaine, an alkaloid derived from the coca-leaf, differs from morphine, codeine and some other opiates in that only relatively small amounts are used worldwide in medical practice. Coca-leaf chewing is traditional and deeply

rooted among large segments of the Andean population, and its use has been associated for centuries with a rich variety of anthropological, social and cultural features. The amounts of coca-leaves required both for licit purposes (the extraction of cocaine for medical purposes and the extraction of a flavouring agent which does not contain any alkaloid) and for chewing represent only a small fraction of the total amount now being produced. This means that most of the production is clearly destined for the illicit manufacture of cocaine and for the illicit traffic. The illicit or uncontrolled growth of the coca bush has created grave problems for States in the Andean region, and burgeoning demand has given rise to illicit traffic and marketing networks in this and other regions.

127. A further important development in international co-operation has been the evolution of a control system for psychotropic substances. Since the 1940s, advances in organic chemistry have resulted in the development of a wide range of synthetic medicaments acting on the central nervous system, and the abuse of many of them has been found to result in drug addiction. Although the controls introduced for narcotic drugs have demonstrated their effectiveness even in the case of those drugs that are manufactured in an entirely synthetic manner and whose number is increasing, the situation is quite different with respect to most psychotropic substances. The response of the international community has been to devise progressively a system of control for psychotropic substances similar to that for narcotic drugs. In view of the diversity of these manufactured substances and their wide applicability and also because the 1971 Convention is a relatively recent instrument, this system of international control has not evolved to the same levels of acceptance and enforcement. Some voluntary measures have been designed that are applied by Governments and have strengthened the control system. Nevertheless, the system has only begun to take effect and diversions from the licit manufacture of certain psychotropic substances under international control and the illicit manufacture of some of them pose a serious threat to the well-being of individual and public health and, moreover, to the national security.

Target 8. Strengthening of the international system of control of narcotic drugs and psychotropic substances

The problem

128. Under article 19 of the 1961 Convention, a State party to the Convention is required to provide to the International Narcotics Control Board (INCB) an annual estimate of the actual amount of narcotic drugs required during the following calendar year. A large number of States have, in addition, undertaken on a voluntary basis to provide similar assessments with respect to psychotropic substances under international control. In some cases estimates have been submitted on the basis of information provided by national pharmaceutical producers or by pharmaceutical companies, which tend to reflect an over-generous appraisal of market potential or excessive prescribing by medical practitioners, or both. Other action is needed to provide more accurate estimates of legitimate medical needs and should include a determination of the therapeutic applications of the narcotic and psychotropic drugs

currently being manufactured and prescribed. Within the context of its Drug Action Programme, WHO has prepared guidelines for more accurate forecasting of requirements for therapeutic use of drugs, including narcotic drugs and psychotropic substances. The improvement of prescription, delivery and utilization practices regarding psychoactive drugs requires an intensification of the co-operation between national pharmaceutical services, medical and pharmaceutical bodies, research institutions, the pharmaceutical industry and others, with a view to ensuring congruence between such practices and the requirements of the international system of controls.

Suggested courses of action

At the national level

129.   The national drug control authority, under the aegis of the appropriate ministry, could gather systematic detailed information and data regarding therapeutic applications of narcotic drugs and psychotropic substances and their preparations from physicians, hospitals, clinics, pharmacists, academic institutions and the pharmaceutical industry as well as from individual manufacturers in order to establish more accurate estimates of the country's legitimate medical needs, work out the annual plan of production and carry out the plan in specific factories assigned by the Government to ensure licit use and prevent abuse.

130.   The authority concerned, in association (as appropriate) with social security agencies, could study the incidence or prevalence of specific diseases treated by the preparations in question.

131.   Professional associations, private foundations and academic institutions, in co-operation with the pharmaceutical industry, and, where appropriate, the ministry of health, should be encouraged to conduct research towards finding less abusable psychoactive drugs which are at least of equal effectiveness and research on combination products where the addition of a counteractive substance leads to products with lower dependence-producing potential. Such research should take fully into account the validity of specific narcotic and psychotropic substances in the management of pain.

132.   In addition, government and non-governmental organizations should be encouraged to conduct scientific studies for the purpose of determining whether equally effective, non-pharmacologic treatment can be developed.

133.   In accordance with the spirit of the Conventions, manufacturers' associations should urge their members to assist the national drug control authority by providing it with data on the quantities actually delivered by manufacturers and distributors to individual bulk consumers.

134.   The national drug control authority, in collaboration with the professional association of pharmacists and social security agencies, could, as appropriate, systematically collect the figures of actual sales of drugs by retail pharmacies.

135. The authority concerned with public health, in consultation with other appropriate authorities, and in accordance with national legislation, could institute a system for monitoring by means of computers or other systems the movement of narcotic drugs and psychotropic substances in the national territory, from the point of manufacture or importation to the point of dispensing in pharmacies, hospitals or offices of medical practitioners.

136. To assist in forecasting national requirements, the national drug control authority, in co-operation with appropriate bodies, could determine the trends in the use of narcotic drugs and psychotropic substances over preceding years and work out projections of their use for the coming three-year period.

At the regional and international levels

137. International organizations or Governments within a region might carry out comparative studies of therapeutic practice in various countries with similar characteristics (such as population, health service and climate), and investigate the reasons for variations in drug use. Such studies ought to be undertaken in co-ordination with appropriate United Nations entities and agencies, such as INCB, the Division of Narcotic Drugs, and WHO.

138. The United Nations should offer to assist Governments with analytical studies of national experiences with regard to the effect of the national drug supply systems on the distribution and availability of narcotic and psychotropic drugs in their countries. Such analyses should also include the effects that international treaty controls have on the distribution, availability and consumption of controlled drugs.

139. The donors of bilateral and multilateral assistance should consider favourably requests by States for financial and other support (including expert advice) for efforts to improve or strengthen national systems for controlling the distribution of narcotic and psychotropic drugs. Such assistance could in the first instance be obtained by authorities of States through technical consultations with the appropriate United Nations entities and agencies and from other Governments with existing effective control systems.

140. Expert meetings should be organized in various regions, on request, by INCB in association with WHO, for the purpose of exchanging experiences in the methodology of forecasting and record-keeping with respect to drug use.

141. The United Nations should ensure that manuals describing the methodologies for estimating requirements of drugs with very high abuse potential are available to all States and that the model INCB reporting forms are available in the official languages and disseminated.

142. The international bodies concerned, in particular WHO, should consider favourably requests by national authorities for assistance in strengthening or establishing a pharmaceutical control agency, under the ministry of health or national authority concerned, for monitoring the manufacture, importation, dispensing and distribution of substances under control. Such assistance could also be provided by Governments with relevant experience and resources.

Target 9. Rational use of pharmaceuticals containing narcotic drugs or psychotropic substances

The problem

143. There is evidence that the supply of essential narcotic drugs and psychotropic substances is not always adequately assured in every country. It is incompatible with the spirit and letter of international drug treaties and with the WHO goal "Health for all by the year 2000" to deprive patients of the necessary and appropriate drug therapy. The identification of national needs and the assurance of an adequate supply of essential drugs are a first priority in any system of health care. At the same time, overuse and misuse of narcotics and psychotropic substances should be avoided.

144. In some countries there are indications that most prescriptions for psychotropic substances are made by medical practitioners who may not be fully aware of the psychotropic properties of these drugs and their potential for misuse and abuse. In addition, these drugs are sometimes prescribed, without thorough evaluation and diagnosis, to a large population of patients for long periods of time without periodic re-evaluation of the need for continuation.

145. In some countries, there are indications that patients are not adequately treated with narcotic drugs and psychotropic substances either initially or for adequate periods of time. While these practices vary among countries, they are often dependent upon the practitioners' knowledge of the various indications for use, appropriate treatment strategies and over-concern for the dependence-producing characteristics of these drugs.

146. The rational use of narcotics and psychotropic substances is frequently hindered by incomplete and often inaccurate data. National health authorities, academic institutions, health professional organizations and others often do not provide adequate information on proper drug use to health professionals. Promotional activities vary in substance and completeness (manufacturers' brochures, advertisements, personal representatives, etc.). In many countries, the monitoring of the prescribing of these substances is poorly organized. There is a need for better statistics and internationally comparable data for the comparative study of trends in the prescribing of drugs. Also, there is a need for improved information on drug use to be made available to health professionals.

147. In some countries, national or international controls inadvertently affect the supply and distribution of drugs, thereby indirectly affecting the availability of these drugs for legitimate medical purposes. This problem has been brought to the attention of and discussed by the WHO Executive Board (EB 79/6, 7 November 1986, paragraphs 17-19). In a number of WHO regions, difficulties have been encountered in obtaining controlled pharmaceuticals. In some cases, pharmacies have become reluctant to stock certain drugs because of the extra record-keeping imposed by national authorities or because inclusion in the Convention on Psychotropic Substances has been interpreted as meaning that the substance is prohibited. This has led to serious problems in availability of these drugs, particularly in rural areas; in primary health care settings such drugs are often no longer available for prescription by health care workers.

This kind of restricted availability can have dire consequences for the proper treatment of serious medical problems and such consequences should not be overlooked.

Suggested courses of action

At the national level

148. The national drug control authority or, as appropriate, the ministry of health could specify, on the basis of needs, the narcotic drugs and psychotropic substances in Schedules II and III which as a minimum must be available for drug therapy in general and for primary health care in particular.

149. The authority concerned, in co-operation with the pharmaceutical industry and with the support of the medical and paramedical professions and pharmacists, as well as with law enforcement agencies, as appropriate, should endeavour to work out agreed guidelines for improving prescription and dispensing practices. National health authorities should ensure that accurate and unbiased information concerning the appropriate use of narcotics and psychoactive substances is made available to health professionals and primary health care workers.

150. National health authorities should also ensure that national and international controls are not misinterpreted so as to limit the availability of narcotic drugs and psychotropic substances for legitimate medical purposes. Where legislation is an impediment to the availability and use of needed drugs, national authorities could give consideration to adopting a more flexible legislative structure.

151. The authority concerned, in co-operation with research and academic institutions, could conduct, or initiate, studies envisaging the monitoring of trends in the prescribing and consumption of psychotropic substances and on their rational use. To improve data collection and analysis, the authority and professional organizations concerned could make use of the WHO Anatomic-Therapeutic-Chemical Drug Classification System and the Defined Daily Doses measurement techniques.

152. For the detection of falsely labelled or low-quality pharmaceutical preparations, either imported or locally manufactured, containing narcotic drugs or psychotropic substances, national pharmaceutical quality control laboratories should be established or strengthened, as necessary. In order to ensure the control of narcotic drugs and psychotropic substances, the activity of national narcotics laboratory services and pharmaceutical control laboratories should be co-ordinated.

153. The ministry of health and, where applicable, other ministries, medical and paramedical professions, manufacturers and other concerned parties, should ensure that the promotion of psychoactive drugs is always based on safety and effectiveness. The ministry of health or any other appropriate authority should regulate the free distribution of samples of narcotic drugs and psychotropic substances.

154. The authority concerned could, as appropriate, review with the pharmaceutical industry or its representative organizations any legislative or voluntary programme concerning any printed or other material publicizing their products, advertisements published or broadcast through mass media and other methods of promoting sales of their pharmaceutical products. The legislative or voluntary programme could make provision for disallowing any exaggerated claims about the stimulative or restorative properties of pharmaceuticals that might tempt drug addicts or potential drug addicts.

At the regional and international levels

155. WHO should promote collaborative research on an international basis, including field research, aimed at providing data to improve drug prescribing and drug consumption. These research efforts should be undertaken both in developing and in developed countries.

156. The appropriate organs of the United Nations should consider co-ordinating studies which assess the availability and utilization of narcotics and psychotropic substances for legitimate medical purposes and which assess the impact of international controls on this availability and use. In the light of the results of these studies, these organs should make recommendations—which may be either of a general character or adapted to the country or region concerned—for improving availability and use and on the need to modify, as appropriate, the international controls of these drugs.

157. WHO should continue to assist national educational authorities to develop training modules for medical and pharmaceutical education and to conduct training courses for medical and other health personnel so as to promote rational prescribing and rational use of pharmaceuticals containing narcotic drugs or psychotropic substances.

Target 10.   Strengthening the control of international movements of psychotropic substances

The problem

158. There is evidence that some lawfully manufactured psychotropic substances are frequently diverted into illicit channels, and the provisions of the 1971 Convention are not adequate to prevent this form of illicit traffic. There are cases in which authorizations for the import of Schedule II psychotropic substances have been falsified and doubts have been cast on the efficacy of the declaration system provided for Schedule III substances. Furthermore, the 1971 Convention does not provide for specific control of international trade in Schedule IV substances. In the absence of an "estimates" system, the only mechanism available to States parties to protect themselves against unwanted shipments is the prohibition provided for in article 13 of the Convention. Inadequate implementation of some provisions of the Convention as well as the absence of national controls in some countries often make the control of the movement of psychotropic substances illusory.

Suggested courses of action

At the national level

159.   To the extent possible, all States should voluntarily extend the system of import and export authorizations provided for in article 12 of the 1971 Convention to cover international trade in substances listed in Schedules III and IV. In addition, immediate action should be taken whenever substances are found to cause significant abuse and/or trafficking problems.

160.   Where medicaments containing psychotropic substances under international control are included in donations for emergency relief in disaster areas, the authorities concerned in the recipient and exporting countries should require that such consignments be authorized for all Schedule II substances and at a minimum be notified to the appropriate authorities with regard to substances in Schedules III and IV, in order that action may be taken to forestall the risk of possible diversion to illicit channels.

At the international level

161.   The parties to the 1971 Convention should consider the possibility of adding to the Convention provisions contemplating the transformation into mandatory measures of the hitherto voluntary measures endorsed by the Economic and Social Council (resolutions 1981/7 and 1985/15) concerning in particular:

   (*a*)   The assessment of legitimate annual needs for Schedule II substances;

   (*b*)   The monitoring by exporting countries of shipments of Schedule IV substances.

162.   The States parties should consider making more general use of the procedure for notification of a national prohibition of and restrictions on the export and import of specific psychotropic substances provided for in article 13 of the 1971 Convention.

163.   Countries that import psychotropic substances, and that need help, should seek assistance from the secretariat of the International Narcotics Control Board, the Division of Narcotic Drugs and the United Nations Fund for Drug Abuse Control in establishing or strengthening national control services.

164.   Countries receiving false or fraudulent permits or orders for psychotropic substances should immediately communicate this fact, together with all known particulars, to the appropriate international organizations such as the INCB and ICPO/Interpol.

165.   Manufacturing and transit countries should, as far as possible, provide the Secretary-General of the United Nations with basic industrial and commercial information regarding sources of supply and movement of psychotropic substances and chemicals and precursors (see also target 12) utilized in the illicit drug traffic, in order to assemble a manageable set of data.

The information could, to the degree possible, be collected, analysed and provided to national enforcement, drug control and customs administrations, taking into consideration the principles of the freedom of trade and the need to safeguard industrial secrets.

Target 11.   Action related to the increase in the number of controlled psychotropic substances

The problem

166.   The number of substances in Schedules III and IV of the 1971 Convention that are used as medicines rose from 15 in 1971 to 60 in 1986, a fourfold increase. These 60 substances are used in hundreds of single and combination products under a variety of trade names. The continuing review process engaged in by WHO will no doubt lead to the addition to the schedules of an even greater number of medically used substances, and the marketing of new psychoactive drugs will necessitate a further extension of the scope of control. There is a genuine need for new psychotropic drugs, and this is one of the reasons for the dynamic psycho-pharmacological research activities being undertaken. About 16 per cent (138) of the 876 drugs launched in 1985 were psychopharmaceuticals, and pharmaceuticals still in research and development were estimated to account for about 21 per cent (851 out of 3,962). Consequently, the list of pharmaceuticals (mainly hypnotics and tranquillizers) will grow even longer in the future. It would be unrealistic to expect that all of these future drugs will be used without the risk of abuse and dependence.

167.   Abuse of substances in Schedules III and IV can in some instances be prevented by pharmaceutical control methods with limited recourse to law enforcement measures. In countries with developed pharmaceutical control services, the control of the entire pharmaceutical supply system can be made more effective. This national pharmaceutical control constitutes the basis for the control of these substances.

Suggested courses of action

At the national level

168.   In view of the fact that the number of psychotropic substances has been steadily increasing during the past few years, and seems certain to continue increasing, each State could elaborate and implement a pharmaceutical policy as a part of its health policy. This would ensure that only medicaments containing psychotropic substances which are necessary for medical care of the population are put on the market. Existing criteria for drug registration should be reviewed and updated, as necessary.

At the international level

169.   National regulations for new drug approval should explicitly state that a test for drug dependence be conducted in the case of a new psychoactive

substance. If it is found to be a potential cause of drug dependence, it should be placed under control so as to prevent its abuse, and WHO should be informed accordingly so that the information can be disseminated.

170. Since the minimum requirements of Schedules III and IV of the 1971 Convention are designed to prevent either the abuse or the likelihood of abuse of the controlled substances to avoid their constituting public health and social problems, the Commission on Narcotic Drugs, in consultation with WHO, should ensure that no undue administrative burdens arise from the control of medically used substances in Schedules III and IV of the 1971 Convention.

171. WHO, in close co-operation with the secretariat of INCB, the Division of Narcotic Drugs and the United Nations Fund for Drug Abuse Control, should consider giving appropriate assistance (if requested) to countries whose pharmaceutical control services are inadequate, in order that these services may be capable of ensuring the control of the manufacture, import, distribution, prescribing and dispensing of psychotropic substances, in accordance with national health policy.

172. WHO might provide international non-proprietary names for the substances included in Schedule I of the 1971 Convention and so far designated by acronyms only.

Target 12. Control of the commercial movement of precursors, specific chemicals and equipment

The problem

173. The continuing increase of the amounts of substances being illegally used for the illicit manufacture of narcotic drugs and psychotropic substances has made it all the more necessary to watch suspect movements of such materials and special equipment used by illicit laboratories. Some of the compounds which are used as precursors for the clandestine manufacture of narcotic drugs are subject to control provisions of the 1961 Convention (for example, ecgonine and thebaine). But there are no provisions in the 1971 Convention which would make possible the scheduling of precursors of psychotropic substances (for example, P^2P, ergotamine, or other lysergic acid derivatives). The prompt reporting of suspect movements of such items would make it easier to discover and apprehend traffickers. Seizures of illicit consignments would also reduce their availability for illicit manufacture. While the use of some specific chemicals is in some cases limited to the manufacture of narcotic drugs or psychotropic substances, other chemicals, and some materials and equipment (for example, tableting and encapsulating machines) are traded and required legitimately in large volume and the shipments should therefore be monitored in such a way as to permit law enforcement intervention with a minimum of burden on legitimate commerce. Particularly strict control measures should, however, be enforced only with respect to those specific chemicals whose use is practically limited to the manufacture of narcotic drugs and psychotropic substances.

Suggested courses of action

At the national level

174. All exports of specifically identified precursors, chemicals and equipment ought to be distinctively, descriptively and accurately labelled and recorded in the exporter's records. A record giving full particulars of the consignee should also be required. Orders which manifestly exceed or are suspected of exceeding normal and legitimate requirements—particularly if the order in question originates in a country where illicit manufacturing is known to take place—should be promptly reported on a voluntary basis to the appropriate drug law enforcement agency by the manufacturer. If reasonable grounds exist for suspecting that the order is illicit, the shipment should be seized by the authorities of the country of origin. Such excessive orders should also be notified promptly to the country of destination and to INCB.

175. As appropriate, in countries where illicit manufacture of narcotic drugs and psychotropic substances occurs, the authority concerned could adopt a system of control over the importation and supply of selected materials and equipment that could be used for such illicit manufacture. If an import order for such items should appear suspect, the said authority could promptly notify the country in which the consignment originates. For the purpose of giving full effect to such system of control, the authority should arrange special training for customs and other law enforcement personnel. Similarly, countries which are sources of such materials and equipment could adopt measures to detect and prevent suspicious shipments as referred to in the preceding paragraph.

176. States should observe and give full effect to the principles embodied in the 1961 and 1971 Conventions which deal with this subject and implement the resolutions on this subject adopted by the Economic and Social Council and by the Commission on Narcotic Drugs, pending entry into force of appropriate international treaty provisions envisaged for inclusion in the new Convention against illicit trafficking.

At the regional and international levels

177. An internationally recognized customs nomenclature should be established under the auspices of CCC for selected precursors, specific chemicals and equipment, and an export consignment including such items should bear a corresponding distinctive and internationally agreed label describing accurately the contents of the consignment.

178. The government agencies concerned could arrange to exchange information regularly and systematically with counterpart agencies in other countries about suspect movements of or transactions in materials and equipment of the kind referred to above and to keep INCB notified accordingly.

179. Joint training courses for customs and other law enforcement officers should be organized by the Division of Narcotic Drugs and other relevant international organizations such as ICPO/Interpol and CCC to familiarize them to the fullest possible extent with the nature of the substances involved and the techniques and *modus operandi* used by traffickers.

180. Governments may wish to consider entering into bilateral or multilateral agreements for the purpose of facilitating exchanges of information and co-operation in this field. In this connection, those negotiating the new draft convention against illicit traffic in narcotic drugs and psychotropic substances could consider the inclusion in that instrument of appropriate clauses making provision for such exchanges and co-operation at the international and regional levels.

Target 13. Control of analogues of substances under international control

The problem

181. Researchers endeavouring to develop a new substance usually identify and study a range of products that have comparable properties but differ slightly in their molecular structure (analogues). They finally select, after a long screening process, the product thought to be the most effective for specific cases and having the least secondary effects. Narcotic drugs and psychotropic substances that are under national and international control are identified by their international or generic names and their chemical formulae. Their analogues, which have not been authorized and are not marketed, though having similar properties are, in many cases, not controlled either by national law or under the international drug control treaties.

182. Unscrupulous persons have, in recent years, produced and distributed through irregular channels some very potent analogues of controlled substances (also referred to as "designer" drugs) in order to circumvent drug laws. These analogues not only pose a serious challenge to drug control, but are highly toxic, contain by-products and impurities and entail a serious threat to health and even to life.

Suggested courses of action

    At the national level

183. Whenever a new analogue is detected on the illicit market, the appropriate authority could be empowered by the legislative authorities to take emergency action to place it under provisional control, with immediate effect.

184. The appropriate authority could prepare draft legislation making it a punishable offence:

    (*a*) To manufacture with the intent to distribute individual analogues of controlled substances for human consumption in non-research environments;

    (*b*) To distribute such analogues.

185. The pharmaceutical control authorities might take action to control analogues of substances under international control and whenever necessary to review the existing criteria for registration and approval of new drugs.

At the international level

186.   The appropriate United Nations agencies should, in conjunction with Governments, review the possible options available for addressing the potential problems of the illicit manufacture and distribution of analogues of controlled substances. Recommendations should be made to the Commission on Narcotic Drugs regarding the most appropriate United Nations mechanism for dealing with this potential problem. Pending such review, any Government having knowledge of a new addictive analogue should promptly notify the Secretary-General accordingly, with a request to communicate the information to other Governments and to WHO.

187.   The Commission on Narcotic Drugs may wish to request the Division of Narcotic Drugs to explore the possibility of developing sensitive and specific detection techniques to detect and identify specific analogues of controlled substances.

Target 14.   Identification of illicit narcotic plant cultivation

The problem

188.   Under the 1961 Convention, article 22, the cultivation of the opium poppy, the coca bush and the cannabis plant is to be prohibited in certain circumstances; this general provision is subject only temporarily and in a few countries to some transitional reservations (article 49). In only one country is opium today produced for licit export. A few countries produce poppy straw for the extraction of opiates for licit use. In a number of countries the opium poppy is cultivated for the production of edible poppy seeds and oil. In some countries there is illicit and uncontrolled production; in certain of the latter countries some production has been traditional. Several States recognize that the successful elimination of this traditional production requires and deserves transitional economic assistance.

189.   The coca bush is grown in countries in and near the Andean region. Under the 1961 Convention, the cultivation of the coca bush is subject to control. The traditional use of its leaves in several of those countries dates from time immemorial. In predominantly farming and mining regions, where leaf-chewing is also practised, there exist deep-rooted cultural, religious and medicinal uses. In recent times the leaf has had licit uses, including the use of a flavouring agent obtained from the leaves after the removal of the alkaloid content. In those countries, growers now sell much of their crop to illicit traffickers, and enormous new acreage has been planted to coca in these and in neighbouring States, all the output of coca leaves being intended exclusively for the illicit market.

190.   Attempts to eliminate illicit production frequently encounter the difficulty of locating sizeable plantations with precision. To avoid detection, growers often place them in remote areas which are very difficult to reach on the surface, often in mountainous terrain, in narrow, steep-walled canyons that are difficult to reach even by air.

191. In a number of regions the most serious handicap for law enforcement agencies is that planting occurs in areas which are difficult to control. The opium poppy, coca bush and cannabis plants are often grown interspersed with other plants, which makes locating and eliminating them even more difficult.

Suggested courses of action

At the national level

192. In order to organize and mount effectively the most appropriate campaign to eliminate the illicit planting of opium poppy, coca bush and cannabis plants, the national authority concerned should make the necessary efforts to obtain maximum international support and use its own internal resources in order:

(*a*) To identify the map co-ordinates of areas under illicit cultivation;

(*b*) To gather data concerning wild growth as well as illicit crops being grown, size of holdings, yields per hectare, labour input and prices obtained by the farmer;

(*c*) To assess land capability (types of soil and soil fertility), climatic factors and land tenure and irrigation systems, to permit selection of substitute crops;

(*d*) To analyse the geographical, political, social and economic conditions of the area in question.

193. At the national level, law enforcement and local government officials, the authority concerned with agriculture and field offices should be consulted, as should organizations and associations of persons likely to have the required information, and aerial photography should be used for spotting clandestine plantations. Each State, subject to respect for the national interest, could report its findings annually to the Commission on Narcotic Drugs in order to facilitate exchange of information among States.

194. In countries in which the cultivation of plants used in the manufacture of narcotics is carried on clandestinely on a large scale, the appropriate authority could, where necessary, conduct a survey with the assistance of the cartographical institute to determine the extent of such cultivation.

195. The survey should, in addition, endeavour to determine how the earnings and mode of life of the rural population concerned would be affected by the discontinuance of illicit cultivation and its replacement by legitimate food or cash crops. Where necessary or desired, assistance might be requested from the United Nations Fund for Drug Abuse Control or other bilateral or multilateral sources for the purpose of carrying out the survey.

196. The appropriate authority in countries where narcotic plants are cultivated illicitly and in areas where rural development assistance is considered appropriate might, after gathering full information on such cultivation, assess the suitability of the land for the planting of legitimate crops, select the crops

best adapted to the environment, and likely to provide the farmers with an adequate livelihood, and work out plans for lessening or eliminating the farmers' dependence on earnings from the sale of illicitly grown plants.

At the regional and international levels

197.   In cases where it is suspected that a sizeable illicit cultivation of the plants in question is carried on but the Government of the territory does not possess the cartographical or other equipment for periodic aerial surveys of suspect areas, that Government could seek co-operation for carrying out such surveys, possibly from a regional or international organization financed by one or more States and/or by the United Nations Fund for Drug Abuse Control.

198.   In this connection, the Secretary-General of the United Nations could convene an expert group meeting composed of experts from countries having the technological capacity for high-resolution satellite imagery and aerial photography and from countries in which illicit cultivation is known to take place. The object of this meeting would be to determine whether and how such technology could be used to detect illicit plantations at the discretion of the country where cultivation is taking place.

Target 15.   Elimination of illicit plantings

The problem

199.   The opium poppy and the cannabis plant can be eradicated by being uprooted or beaten down manually or mechanically, by being sprayed manually (i.e. using back packs) with herbicides and, if the plantations are sufficiently large and the terrain permits, by being sprayed aerially. They may also be eliminated in connection with programmes of transitional economic assistance. The eradication efforts might also be co-ordinated with long-term integrated development projects accompanied by law enforcement activities, as appropriate.

200.   Manual or mechanical uprooting is often hampered by the rugged nature or inaccessibility of the terrain; besides, the process is inefficient and slow, especially if many areas are to be cleared, and furthermore in some areas law enforcement officers who are present on the spot may be risking their lives. These considerations apply also to manual or back-pack spraying. In developing countries these eradication techniques may require a larger deployment of scarce resources than does aerial spraying.

201.   In certain circumstances, aerial spraying may be considered appropriate: it involves the use of suitable aircraft, adequately qualified pilots, and carefully tested herbicides which do not cause any harm to human beings or to the environment. Aerial spraying may be inadvisable where the plants in question are interspersed with other plantings or are grown in small numbers or near populated areas. Fixed- and rotary-wing aircraft are commonly used in agriculture and are efficient for spraying large fields from the air.

202. Any chemical used in spraying must be proved to be harmless to human beings and to the particular environment. The International Code of Conduct on the distribution and use of pesticides, adopted by resolution 10/85 of the 23rd FAO Conference, could provide useful guidance in this regard. All the herbicides utilized in illicit crop eradication are widely employed in commercial agriculture and are generally registered for use in major agricultural countries. Some herbicides utilized for commercial range and brush control are partially effective against coca. Research is currently being sponsored to develop a herbicide, or herbicide application technique, which is fully effective in all the major growing environments.

203. Some States in the Middle East and Asia had tolerated the cultivation of the opium poppy under circumstances which lead certain States to believe that the growers, if now required to abandon these plantations, should be given transitional economic assistance. Similar considerations may apply also to certain traditional growers of coca in the Andean region. Rural development of the areas, improved roads, schools, medical treatment, adult education and literacy programmes, advice on other crops, fertilizers and the like can help persuade the former growers to comply with the ban on cultivation; appropriate opportunity should be given for an initial phase of voluntary eradication prior to the imposition of compulsory measures.

204. International co-operation for rural development or crop substitution should be conditional upon States adhering to eradication targets, so far as possible, within mutually agreed time schedules, in conformity with the obligations under the 1961 Convention. An effective crop reduction or eradication programme would require:

(a) Surveys of the project area conducted jointly by United Nations executing agencies and interested States to determine the success of the programme;

(b) Monitoring, by the State concerned, of the area where crops have been destroyed and where substitute crops are cultivated, to clarify that there is no illegal replanting of poppy, coca or cannabis.

205. Transitional economic co-operation may also be used by some countries in the context of a programme for the eradication of existing illicit crops and the prevention of the extension of the illicit growth of narcotic plants.

Suggested courses of action

At the national level

206. If they have designated the co-ordinating agency referred to in article 35(a) of the 1961 Convention and article 21(a) of the 1971 Convention, States parties to these instruments might as a first step direct the agency to prepare and keep up to date a comprehensive plan for the elimination of the illicitly cultivated narcotic plants that have been discovered (see target 14):

(a) **Opium poppy.** Where a sizeable illicit growth of opium poppy has been discovered, the extent of the plantings, their physical accessibility and local political conditions might be investigated. A campaign might then be prepared to eliminate them in the manner most appropriate in the circumstances. Aerial spraying is efficient if the fields are large enough, if equipment, pilots and funds are available and if the chemical to be used has been found to be environmentally safe on the terrain. Alternatively, arrangements could be made to have personnel on the spot in good time to uproot or spray the plantations manually. If the country concerned is one of those that believe that such plantings can be eliminated in a reasonably short time through a programme of transitional economic assistance or that eradication should be accompanied by transitional economic assistance in the growing area, such a programme might be planned and appropriate technical and financial assistance sought, if needed. Any transitional economic assistance could be contingent on commitment to the complete abandonment of illicit cultivation. The ban could be imposed in stages;

(b) **Coca bush.** States in whose territories sizeable plantations of coca bush have been discovered could proceed along lines similar to those suggested above for opium poppy. Since the coca bush has been cultivated and coca leaves have been chewed for centuries in some parts of the Andean region, and in some of them the practice continues, transitional economic assistance and phased elimination of coca growing may be important in some areas;

(c) **Cannabis plant.** States in whose territories sizeable plantations of illicit cannabis have been discovered could proceed along the lines outlined above. Much of the illicit cannabis is grown on very small plots that are not easy to find and cannot be aerially sprayed.

At the regional and international levels

207. The Division of Narcotic Drugs, working in close collaboration with the international bodies concerned, should encourage States to report on their efforts to locate and to eliminate the illicit cultivation of narcotic plants in their annual report to the Secretary-General, updated summaries of which should be communicated to the Commission on Narcotic Drugs. The United Nations Fund for Drug Abuse Control should continue to encourage and help States to develop master plans for narcotics control, including the elimination of illicit crops.

208. The Secretary-General, in consultation with States where the illicit cultivation takes place and with other concerned States, should consider convening a study group of specially selected experts, including experts of the States directly concerned to study and recommend environmentally safe methods for eradicating illicit plants. The United Nations Environment Programme (UNEP), WHO, FAO and the United Nations Fund for Drug Abuse Control may be invited to participate in the study. Special attention should be given to appraising herbicides for use in safely eradicating illicit plantations of the three narcotic plants, in the various environments and conditions likely to be encountered. In particular, attention should be paid to determining which herbicides would be safe to human beings and effective against illicit cultivation by spraying from the air and at ground level. In this connection, the resources of the International Register on Potentially Toxic Chemicals (IRPTC)—a UNEP data base located in Geneva—can prove particularly helpful.

209.   The authorities concerned of States that have the material, technological and financial capability to offer to the corresponding ministries of other States, particularly developing States, co-operation in carrying out measures of eradicating illicitly cultivated narcotic crops might co-operate with those other States at their request and, if appropriate, offer to supply chemical or like substances for use in the eradication measures. Requests for such co-operation might be transmitted directly to the United Nations Fund for Drug Abuse Control.

Target 16.   Redevelopment of areas formerly under illicit drug crop cultivation

The problem

210.   Narcotic plants can be, and often are, cultivated on marginal land in remote areas; they do not require specialized agricultural skills or costly inputs. The expense of transporting narcotic products is almost irrelevant, because of their high value per unit weight. Although the grower's income from the sale of the narcotic plants represents only a small fraction of the money that changes hands in the illicit trafficking and distribution of the drugs, the grower's earnings from these crops are generally higher than those from any alternative food or cash crops that can be identified as being suitable for cultivation on the same land area.

211.   The reduction of illicit cultivation through law enforcement measures may affect the income of the farming communities concerned and in some cases leave the farmers in the short term without any means of subsistence. Accordingly, the Government may wish to consider undertaking in the traditional growing areas a programme that would assist these farmers in raising crops other than narcotic plants and/or in seeking other means of livelihood. Experience shows that such programmes are most effective if they form part of more general comprehensive rural development programmes offering, for example, improved infrastructure, credit, and marketing facilities. Integrated rural development and crop substitution involve a multidisciplinary and integrated approach to change from traditional low-income and low-input agriculture to a more broadly based economy with higher technology and involving alternative cash crops as well as other sources of income. Any rural redevelopment scheme of this kind should, of course, be closely supervised lest it inadvertently give some benefit or advantage to drug traffickers. Moreover, to be successful these development efforts must be accompanied by effective enforcement, including bans on cultivation and effective interdiction both within the compass of the rural development programme itself and beyond.

Suggested courses of action

   At the national level

212.   The national authorities concerned could:

   (*a*)   Carry out market surveys followed by in-depth studies, where necessary, aimed at identifying domestic and export markets for substitute crops and determining the feasibility of setting up product-processing facilities, possibly with the participation of the private sector;

(*b*)   Strengthen agricultural research and extension in areas growing illicit drug crops with a view to determining the short-term and long-term requirements of any crop substitution programmes envisaged, for example as regards input needs, plant population, harvesting techniques and marketing of the harvest. Long-term research would also cover seed-bed preparation, efficient use of irrigation, dry farming techniques etc.;

(*c*)   Develop the infrastructure with a view to creating an improved living environment for the farmer, in support of government efforts to eliminate illicit cultivation, including, for example, improvement of health and sanitary conditions, launching adult education programmes and literacy campaigns, provision of educational facilities, road construction and other initiatives that would take into account the remoteness and isolation of the drug-producing areas in general.

At the regional and international levels

213.   Regional bodies should co-ordinate the actions of Governments at regional or subregional levels for the purpose of identifying areas formerly under illicit cultivation that cut across national boundaries and that may be suitable for redevelopment, having regard to the different crops grown in the region.

214.   An international campaign with the participation of the United Nations family of organizations and other regional and international organizations should be undertaken to increase the flow of resources to programmes that are designed to reduce the supply of drugs through rural development, crop substitution, agricultural and industrial development, educational programmes, research and extension activities.

215.   International intergovernmental and non-governmental bodies interested in this field should set up training and information activities and prepare materials to this end, including video films and material based on other advanced techniques, in support of the programmes aimed at recommending alternative crops or other means of livelihood for farmers in areas in which narcotic plants are grown illicitly.

216.   International assistance should be granted to the countries concerned in the form of financing provided by the international community through the United Nations Fund for Drug Abuse Control or other channels. Donors to UNFDAC should be encouraged to increase their contributions to enable the Fund to expand the scope of its activities.

217.   In cases where an area previously used by the resident rural population for the illicit cultivation of opium poppy or coca plants or cannabis has been transformed into land planted to substitute crops for which there is a potential export market, the Governments of countries that may offer an outlet for such substitute crops might consider favourably the grant of preferential tariff and non-tariff treatment to imports of produce grown on such converted land. For this purpose, the importing and exporting countries concerned may consider it

desirable to enter into agreements stipulating the precise conditions and specifying the commodities in question and the nature of the preferences granted.

218.   International financing institutions should contribute more extensively to integrated rural development in support of the eradication of illicit plantings and crop substitution programmes, if the countries concerned so request.

219.   Where illicit cultivation of opium poppy, coca bush or cannabis plant occurs on a considerable scale, development co-operation in a project should be subject to mutual agreement by the co-operating parties. The provision of co-operation funds should be based on mutually agreed terms which could include crop reduction, crop substitution or other methods designed to eliminate illicit cultivation of the said plants.

220.   Government agencies and international institutions should exchange information on progress in crop substitution in the course of deliberations on agricultural and integrated rural development in the international forums concerned.

221.   The results of successful integrated rural development (IRD) and crop substitution programmes should be made generally available with a view to encouraging other countries to undertake similar programmes where needed. Data on both successful and unsuccessful experiences should be gathered and analysed by FAO, with a view to elaborating an improved methodology for integrated rural development and crop substitution. United Nations organizations, including the regional commissions, which deal with various aspects of IRD (e.g., popular participation, women's and youths' access to productive roles, and intra-governmental and inter-agency co-operation) should give explicit attention to the problems associated with illicit drug production. UNFDAC and the United Nations regional commissions should examine the possibilities of joint co-ordination of such efforts.

222.   In view of the marked rise in illicit demand for drugs in a number of developing countries where, until recently, drug abuse had not been on a serious scale, the government agencies concerned in donor countries and the governing bodies of intergovernmental financial institutions might take into account in their development assistance programmes the desirability of supporting or promoting in those developing countries, with their concurrence, economic and other projects or activities that would help to curb the rise in drug abuse and/or illicit drug production in those countries. Projects and activities of this kind might include integrated agricultural, industrial or rural development schemes, more comprehensive in scope than mere crop substitution schemes. While the emphasis to be given in bilateral or multilateral development assistance programmes to projects specifically designed to discourage the growth of illicit demand for drugs is bound to vary from case to case and according to the preferences of the Governments of countries where the projects are being carried out, the donors of financial and other assistance should, as far as possible, co-ordinate the flow and composition of assistance in such a way as to make an impact on drug abuse. In this respect, the United Nations Fund for Drug Abuse Control is performing a valuable co-ordinating function.

Chapter III

SUPPRESSION OF ILLICIT TRAFFICKING

Introduction

223.   Drug trafficking is sophisticated and complex. A wide variety of drugs is involved, and they may be of external or domestic origin. The illicit traffic in drugs not only violates national drug laws and international conventions, but may in many cases also involve other antisocial activities, such as organized crime, conspiracy, bribery, corruption and intimidation of public officials, tax evasion, banking law violations, illegal money transfers, criminal violations of import or export regulations, crimes involving firearms, and crimes of violence. Narcotics are now frequently used instead of money as a medium of exchange for trading in weapons and other contraband, and some large drug-trafficking networks have gained virtual control of certain areas. Because of the far-reaching consequences of the illicit drug trade, even the integrity and stability of certain Governments have been threatened. This wide range of illegal activities presents an equally wide range of openings for imaginative law enforcement action, including action recognizing the need to develop and implement law enforcement programmes relating to subjects identified in the draft convention against illicit drug trafficking and to give emphasis to the recommendations of the Interregional Meeting of Heads of National Drug Law Enforcement Agencies, as reflected in the report of the Meeting (A/41/559).

224.   Action on the lines suggested in chapter I, concerning the prevention and reduction of illicit demand, and in chapter II, on the elimination of illicit supply, would obviously go a long way towards suppressing illicit trafficking.

225.   In addition, however, it is necessary to ensure vigorous enforcement of the law in order to reduce the illicit availability of drugs, deter drug-related crime, and contribute to drug abuse prevention by creating an environment favourable to efforts for reducing illicit supply and demand. The challenge is to overcome the obstacles posed by the complexity of international transactions, the covert nature of the drug traffic and the large sums of money to be made from illicit drugs in proportion to their often low bulk. Co-ordination of activities and co-operation among national agencies within each country and between countries are vital for the achievement of the objective.

226.   Many Governments have initiated innovative methods for disrupting drug-trafficking organizations. These successful initiatives may usefully be shared with other Governments, where applicable, and can be adapted to the particular situation in a given area or region.

227.   Special emphasis should be placed on supplementing the activities of the police and customs authorities by increasing the effectiveness of the criminal justice system in the arrest, prosecution and appropriate sentencing of convicted traffickers. The support of the full range of non-governmental organizations that have an interest in law enforcement and judicial matters should also be enlisted. Mutual legal and judicial assistance between national jurisdictions should be fostered and facilitated, as should co-operation between law enforcement agencies. Assets gained from the illicit drug trade should be made liable to seizure, as should the instruments used in trafficking. The extradition from one country of persons accused of drug offences in another country should be facilitated to the extent that it is not incompatible with the existing national legislation of the countries concerned.

228.   An important step now being taken by the international community in this regard is the drafting of a new convention against illicit traffic in narcotic drugs and psychotropic substances,[3] which is being prepared under the auspices of the Commission on Narcotic Drugs at the request of the General Assembly and which it is hoped will be adopted in the near future. States are encouraged to take an active part in the elaboration of the new convention and to become parties to the convention once it has been adopted. Pending its entry into force, which may take some time, measures envisaged in the proposed new convention could be taken to the extent possible by, when necessary, the introduction of appropriate provisions into national law.

229.   Ratification and effective implementation by all States of the international conventions relating to drug abuse control will greatly enhance the prospects of ridding the world of illicit drug trafficking.

230.   The international intergovernmental bodies concerned should bring to the attention of Governments any deficiencies noted in the operation of the international drug control system (e.g. leakages into illicit channels), and invite them to suggest or consider making (as the case may be) efforts to remedy the shortcomings at the national, regional and international levels.

Target 17.   Disruption of major trafficking networks

The problem

231.   Timely information on the criminal activities of traffickers is required in order that they can be identified and caught. Such information is often available in the records of organizations such as banks, air, road, rail and maritime transportation companies, managements of ports and airports, free-port authorities, courier services, money changers and financial and investment houses. Personnel in all organizations concerned should be trained to recognize the value to law enforcement authorities of such information.

232.   The object is to channel all pertinent information to the appropriate law enforcement agencies promptly so that traffickers can be identified and caught.

---

[3]See the report on the first session (A/CONF.133/PC/6).

It is therefore necessary to strengthen co-operation between law enforcement agencies within each State and, under bilateral agreements, between these and their counterparts in other States, enhance training of law enforcement personnel (in skill and integrity) and enlist the assistance of the non-governmental sector in gathering information.

233.   For this purpose, States parties that have not yet done so are urged to designate the co-ordinating agency envisaged in article 35(*a*) of the 1961 Convention and article 21(*a*) of the 1971 Convention, which should be given the necessary authority to co-ordinate the actions set forth below.

Suggested courses of action

   At the national level

234.   Having due regard to the national administrative and legal system, the agency could gather from all government agencies information useful for drug law enforcement and, subject to respect for privacy and confidentiality, ensure that this information is communicated promptly to the appropriate law enforcement agency; this requirement could, if necessary, be spelt out in appropriate laws and regulations.

235.   The ministry or authority concerned could be made responsible for arranging training for the personnel of all such agencies to enable them to recognize and to transmit promptly to the appropriate agency any information useful for the purpose of identifying traffickers and detecting their activities.

236.   The appropriate agency could approach air and rail transport firms and shipping and trucking firms which operate internationally, and/or the associations of such firms, urging them to review their procedures for the purpose not only of safeguarding their services against misuse by traffickers (see also target 24) but also of ensuring that information about any trafficking operation whatsoever is reported promptly.

237.   Legislative bodies could consider enacting legislation applying penalties to transport companies that are aware of such misuse and illicit traffic and do not take prompt and adequate steps to correct and report it or are reckless or grossly negligent in this regard. Legislation providing in such circumstances for the seizure and immobilization of transport equipment used in drug trafficking could be enacted if not already in effect (see also target 23).

238.   Subject to the limitations necessitated by the constitutional, legal and administrative system, the appropriate ministry or other national authority responsible for financial matters should ensure that any suspect activity by banks, money changers, financial and investment houses and courier and related services is promptly reported to the ministry or authority concerned and to the drug law enforcement agency. Similarly, in cases where information held by the tax authorities might assist investigations, this information could be made accessible to the drug law enforcement agency. Any amendment needed in banking and corporate secrecy laws should be in terms conducive to the discovery of drug-related offences. With the support or advice of the ministry

or authority, training courses might be arranged for the staff of banking and financial institutions, so that they can learn how to recognize suspect transactions. The movement of unusually large amounts of cash or negotiable instruments, the deposit of exceptionally large amounts of cash in banks, the unreported maintenance of accounts abroad by nationals or residents in cases where such amounts are required to be reported, and large unexplained accumulations of wealth of obviously illicit origin should by law be liable to penalties if there is evidence of "laundering" or concealment of funds connected with illicit drug trafficking.

239.   The appropriate ministry or other appropriate authority at the local level could establish standards of conduct and integrity for law enforcement agencies and officers that are involved in drug law enforcement. All States should ensure that an appropriate legal framework with penal sanctions is enacted (if they do not already exist) to support the criminal prosecution and punishment of corruption offences.

240.   The appropriate national authorities could, with due regard for the fundamental principles of the national legal system, make use of all modern techniques of investigation in the fight against organized international drug trafficking, including corruption offences by public officials.

241.   If in the course of investigating suspect activities a government agency discovers evidence of a connection between illicit drug trafficking and illicit arms trafficking or international organized criminal activities, it should promptly inform other national authorities accordingly and communicate relevant particulars to the authority concerned in the country that is the probable target of the illicit traffic or organized criminal activity in question.

At the regional and international levels

242.   The ministries concerned and national law enforcement agencies should, as appropriate, under international treaties and bilateral agreements co-operate closely with their counterparts in other States and in liaison with ICPO/Interpol when appropriate with a view to enhancing the effectiveness of their law enforcement action to suppress the illicit drug traffic. For this purpose, they could establish and maintain channels of communication between their respective law enforcement agencies, by means of which information can be exchanged without delay.

243.   States should endeavour, directly or through the appropriate international organizations, to establish regional and international agreements strengthening co-operation in the fight against the illicit drug traffic.

244.   Bilateral and multilateral assistance should be sought, where needed, for the purpose of financing programmes of technical co-operation and assistance and improving channels of communication for the transmission of information relating to the fight against the illicit drug traffic.

245.   With the co-operation of ICPO/Interpol and CCC, when appropriate, the Division of Narcotic Drugs should continue to organize regular regional

and interregional training courses to train personnel of law enforcement and related agencies and officials of national tourist agencies and to promote co-operation among these agencies in the fight against the illicit drug traffic.

246.   Since the operations of drug trafficking gangs may vary from region to region, information available on profiles and methods of operation could be gathered by national authorities at the regional level in co-operation with ICPO/Interpol and CCC, when appropriate, to be used by States as well as by international agencies and entities concerned.

247.   In countries where it is known or suspected that the "informal" or "parallel" sector of the economy accounts for a significant share of the national product and of international trade, the appropriate ministry or authority might investigate the ways in which the illicit production of and traffic in drugs contribute to the "informal" economic activities and take counteraction. The ministry or the authority concerned may wish to communicate the relevant information to other countries, in the region or elsewhere, which are known destinations of the illicit cross-border drug traffic or of the flight of assets representing earnings of traffickers from unlawful transactions.

248.   If conclusive evidence comes to light of illicit trafficking being carried on by means of the misuse of the diplomatic bag or of the diplomatic status, or of the consular status, it is open to the Government of the receiving State to take measures for halting this traffic and for dealing with the diplomatic or consular staff involved in strict conformity with the provisions of the Vienna Conventions on Diplomatic and Consular Relations.[4] The Conference draws the attention of the International Law Commission to possible misuse of the diplomatic bag for illicit drug trafficking, so that the Commission could study the matter under the topic relating to the status of the diplomatic bag.

Target 18.   Promoting use of the technique of controlled delivery

The problem

249.   The law enforcement technique of controlled delivery is widely considered to be an efficient tool in identifying and neutralizing major organizers of international drug trafficking. This procedure involves allowing a delivery of illicit drugs, once detected, to proceed, under constant and secret surveillance, to the ultimate destination envisaged by the traffickers, the object of the surveillance being to lead to the discovery and eventual arrest of the trafficking ringleaders. Difficulties have arisen in some national jurisdictions, where legislative provisions require the suspect's immediate arrest upon detection, and also where the responsibility for such surveillance is ill-defined and the strict enforcement of penal law by the country of destination is not guaranteed or where the penalty for trafficking is lax or less stringent. In addition, there is a risk that the shipment may escape into illicit hands. High operational costs, and the non-availability of trained staff, have in some countries inhibited the use of this most useful method of tracing the delivery of illicit drugs to the ultimate destination.

---

[4]*United Nations Treaty Series*, vol. 500, No. 7310 and vol. 596, No. 8638.

Suggested courses of action

   At the national level

250.   Unless the constitution of the State concerned rules out the amendment of the law in such a way as to permit the use of the technique of controlled delivery, consideration should be given to amending the law so as to permit its use following prior bilateral agreements or arrangements. The legislature and the appropriate ministry or authorities could take the necessary measures pursuant to domestic law to authorize the appropriate use of the technique of controlled delivery for the purpose of identifying and bringing to justice the individuals, corporations or other organizations involved in the shipment, transportation, delivery, concealment or receipt of an illicit consignment of controlled substances that might not be detected if the intermediaries or couriers were arrested immediately on identification.

   At the regional and international levels

251.   In order to ensure that controlled delivery is being effectively co-ordinated at both national and international levels, States could, if they consider it appropriate, designate an agency or agencies as responsible for such co-ordination.

252.   With the assistance of the United Nations Fund for Drug Abuse Control and in close co-operation with ICPO/Interpol and CCC, the Division of Narcotic Drugs should organize regional training courses for law enforcement and judicial officers for the purpose of drawing up guidelines and instructing them in techniques of surveillance, control, and co-ordination of controlled delivery.

Target 19.   Facilitation of extradition

The problem

253.   Despite the community of interests and obligations shared by the States parties to the 1961 and 1971 Conventions, the laws and regulations concerning persons accused of drug-related offences vary considerably from one country to another. These differences in legislations provide traffickers with opportunities for evading capture and trial; for example, the traffickers may be resident in a country whose law or administration of justice is so lax that they enjoy virtual immunity from prosecution or from extradition to a country in which they are accused of a criminal offence.

254.   It would obviously be a strong deterrent to traffickers if they knew that prosecution, trial and, if convicted, punishment for drug-related offences would be inescapable, and that extradition to the country in which the alleged offence was committed and which asks for extradition would be almost certain, subject to observance of the proper national legal procedure. The enactment of

appropriate legislation where it does not already exist, and its strict enforcement, would go a long way towards denying drug traffickers any haven of refuge.

Suggested courses of action

At the national level

255. If the appropriate national authority deems it necessary, the national legislation could be reviewed to ensure that each of the acts enumerated in paragraph 273, be defined as extraditable offences and included (by amendment if necessary) in existing and in contemplated extradition treaties.

At the regional and international levels

256. States could consider entering into bilateral or multilateral extradition treaties concerning drug trafficking and other related offences if they deem this to be appropriate.

Target 20. Mutual judicial and legal assistance

The problem

257. The multinational aspects of illicit trafficking in drugs greatly complicate law enforcement, investigation and judicial counteraction. Witnesses, documents and other evidence are often scattered in States other than the State in which persons accused of drug-related offences are brought to trial, and the detailed rules concerning the production of evidence can create difficulties for judicial bodies. Subject to the limitations of the constitutional, legal and administrative system, needed mutual legal assistance includes, for example:

(*a*) Taking evidence, including compelling testimony;

(*b*) Serving judicial documents;

(*c*) Executing requests for searches and seizures;

(*d*) Examining objects, sites and conveyances;

(*e*) Locating or identifying witnesses or suspects;

(*f*) Verifying in narcotics laboratories the illegal nature of substances seized;

(*g*) Exchanging information and objects;

(*h*) Providing relevant documents and records, including bank, financial, corporate and business records: existing bank secrecy laws are being used in many instances to obstruct co-operation and the provision of information needed for the investigation of allegations of drug-related offences.

Suggested courses of action

At the national level

258.   The appropriate authorities could suggest that, in conformity with the relevant bilateral and multilateral agreements, the greatest possible measure of mutual judicial assistance should be provided in judicial proceedings, including investigations and prosecutions relating to illicit trafficking offences, making or proposing any necessary modifications in the legislation, regulations or procedures. Legislative provisions could be enacted as required, granting broad powers to the courts to assist courts in other jurisdictions in gathering evidence in accordance with the laws of the requested State and, to the greatest extent possible, in conformity with the laws of the requesting State.

259.   Each State could ensure that the appropriate agency or responsible authority has the capacity to receive requests for mutual legal assistance and to address such requests to other States. The agency or authority of the requested State should have capacity to recommend that requests for mutual legal assistance be executed in accordance with the procedural requirements specified in the request in so far as they are not incompatible with the law of the requested State.

At the regional and international levels

260.   The appropriate ministries or authorities could, in co-operation with ministries of foreign affairs, initiate action to enter into regional or inter-national agreements that would serve the purposes described above. A number of States have entered into or are negotiating bilateral and regional agreements for these purposes. Many such agreements relax the rules governing bank secrecy in drug trafficking cases, thus reducing the number of "safe havens" available to traffickers.

261.   The Secretary-General of the United Nations should be requested by the Commission on Narcotic Drugs to issue periodically lists of the national agencies or authorities designated by States parties to facilitate legal and judicial co-operation.

262.   The Secretary-General should also be requested to publish a compendium of the bilateral and regional agreements on mutual legal assistance entered into by States, and States should report the conclusion of such agreements to the Secretary-General, if the Parties deem this to be appropriate.

263.   In view of the paramount importance of timely intelligence in the fight against illicit trafficking, Governments would be able to intensify their efforts against these illicit activities if they possessed efficient channels of communica-tion enabling them to track movements of traffickers promptly. For this purpose they may find it useful to enter into multilateral, bilateral or regional arrangements providing for the reciprocal exchange of relevant information among law enforcement agencies, including those of transit States. The latter may request assistance from the United Nations Fund for Drug Abuse Control

and bilateral and multilateral assistance programmes in establishing or expanding their communications network for this purpose.

264. In cases where they consider it desirable with a view to strengthening international or regional peace and security and building confidence, interested Governments might envisage the conclusion of formal agreements (in so far as these do not already exist) that contain provisions for pursuing the fight against illicit drug trafficking. Such agreements might envisage, *inter alia*, reciprocal training courses for officials, greater ease of communication between authorities, the establishment of direct telex links etc.

265. States whose systems of law and rules of evidence and procedure are much alike may wish to consider entering into agreements for the transfer of criminal proceedings as appropriate and for the reciprocal recognition of judicial decisions concerning drug-related offences. In such cases, the provisions of such an agreement might specify that the order of the court in one State party to the agreement is enforceable in another State party, provided that in cases where a sentence is imposed the respect of the convicted person's fundamental human rights is guaranteed in the place where the sentence is to be served.

Target 21. Admissibility in evidence of samples of bulk seizures of drugs

The problem

266. Frequently, law enforcement authorities seize an illicit shipment of drugs of considerable bulk. Laws and regulations in some States require the holding of that entire bulk shipment pending the completion of investigation and trial. During the waiting period there is a risk that the seized drugs might again leak into the illicit traffic. Also, some States lack adequate laboratories for the analysis of the seizure; yet accurate and timely analysis is essential to the successful prosecution of drug-related offences. Technical methodologies need to be established for the safe destruction of bulk seizures of drugs as well as for the accurate chemical analysis of samples, including the determination of adequate procedures for taking samples from bulk seizures.

Suggested courses of action

At the national level

267. Within the scope of the fundamental principles of the national legal system, legislation could be enacted or amended, as appropriate, to authorize the early destruction or other lawful disposal of seizures of narcotic drugs and psychotropic substances after the legally required sample or samples have been taken for analysis and evidentiary purposes. In any event, security procedures should, as necessary, be introduced and maintained for the safe storage and disposal of seized drugs to ensure that no part of the seizure is diverted into the illicit market.

268. In States lacking adequate capabilities for carrying out chemical or forensic analyses, every effort should be made to establish such laboratories; in the absence of such facilities, the law may empower the judiciary to admit in evidence the analytical findings of foreign laboratories recognized by the Government. Such laboratories may include but should not be limited to those of the appropriate international bodies or those established on a regional basis. Furthermore, in some cases, it may be desirable to permit use of the mails to ship, in a controlled manner, samples of seized narcotics and psychotropic substances to regional or other laboratories for analysis.

At the regional and international levels

269. The Division of Narcotic Drugs should continue to give high priority, with the assistance of UNFDAC, to its programme of scientific and technical assistance and should give full support to the establishment and strengthening of national and regional narcotics laboratories in States having limited resources and affected by the illicit production, trafficking, transit or consumption of drugs of abuse.

270. The Division should work out acceptable standardized methods for carrying out analyses of seized narcotic and psychotropic material, continue to serve as a central source of pure reference standards and establish universally recognized forms for the submission of results of analyses of seizures. In this connection, increased co-operation for the exchange, pooling and dissemination of information, for example relating to methods of analysis, new trends, non-controlled substances of abuse and source of manufacture, should be promoted.

Target 22. Adequacy with a view to improved efficacy of penal provisions

The problem

271. Articles 36 and 22 of the 1961 and 1971 Conventions respectively provide that acts contravening the provisions of those Conventions are to be declared punishable offences by States parties to them. Because definitions of drug-related offences and the penal provisions are not uniform but may vary from country to country, there are loopholes by which drug traffickers and their accomplices can escape prosecution. Sentencing practices also vary widely within and between national jurisdictions, as do policies regarding conditional release after arrest and after sentences involving deprivation of liberty.

Suggested courses of action

At the national level

272. The legislature, ministries or other authorities concerned, university faculties of law, research institutions and like academic bodies, might review

national law and practice to ensure that illicit drug production and trafficking offences are punishable by adequate measures.

273. Within the scope of the fundamental principles of the national legal system, States might take necessary measures to establish as offences under criminal law:

(a) The illicit production, trafficking, or importation of narcotic drugs or psychotropic substances;

(b) The manufacture, distribution, possession or temporary possession of materials or equipment intended for use in the illicit production or manufacture of narcotic drugs or of psychotropic substances;

(c) The acquisition, possession, temporary possession, transfer or laundering of proceeds or instrumentalities derived from or used in illicit traffic;

(d) Conspiracy to commit, attempts to commit and participation in the commission of the said offences.

274. States could ensure, by legislation if appropriate, that their judicial system takes into consideration, in connection with initial sentencing and eventual parole, aggravating circumstances which may include, *inter alia:*

(a) The involvement of the planners and organizers of organized criminal groups;

(b) The use of firearms or violence;

(c) The fact that the offender holds public office or is a medical practitioner;

(d) Previous drug trafficking offences, wherever committed;

(e) The manifest intent of the offender to infiltrate and introduce drugs into closed institutions such as prisons, military premises, boarding schools, treatment and rehabilitation centres for drug addicts and the like, and to employ minors in furtherance of the commission of the offence;

(f) The victimization of minors.

275. States may wish to ensure that their judicial authorities observe the utmost caution in granting to an alleged offender conditional release on bail or bond after arrest and pending trial, for traffickers command such large resources that they can easily afford losses arising from any bail or bond forfeiture. As drug trafficking offences are usually part of a continuing criminal enterprise, States could provide a legal basis for denying conditional release when there is evidence that such release would constitute a continuing threat to the community.

276. The appropriate ministry or authority could propose legislation (in so far as it does not already exist) providing disciplinary or penal measures with respect to any medical prescriber who is proved to have accepted financial or other favours in return for prescriptions. Similar measures would be applicable to any medical practitioners who are proved to have prescribed inappropriate medicaments to persons known to them to be drug addicts or as being likely to divert the drugs prescribed to the illicit traffic. Analogous provisions would be applicable to pharmacists and nurses in cases of improper dispensing.

At the regional and international levels

277.   For the purpose of promoting concerted efforts to deter traffickers from exploiting the diversity of laws and sentencing practices and penal prosecution in countries in a particular region, the Governments and legislatures should encourage greater co-operation among judicial, police and customs authorities and should consider to what extent the divers laws, sentencing practices and penal prosecution concerning illicit trafficking may be harmonized at the regional level and effectively implemented at the national level.

Target 23.   Forfeiture of the instruments and proceeds of illicit drug trafficking

The problem

278.   In line with the provisions of article 37 of the 1961 Convention and article 22, paragraph 3, of the 1971 Convention referring to objects directly associated with the commission of a drug trafficking offence, most national criminal or civil legal systems make provision for the seizure and forfeiture of the tools and devices actually used in committing the offence. Most of such existing provisions, however, cannot be construed as being applicable to assets acquired by means of the proceeds resulting from drug trafficking.

279.   The volume of the property and money transactions, and especially of cash transfers, related to drug trafficking has increased so greatly that these transactions affect some national economies in their entirety. The increased use by traffickers and their associates of complex corporate structures and intricate business transactions involving banks, trust companies, firms dealing in real estate and other financial institutions has added to the difficulty of seizing assets obtained as a result of trafficking in drugs. Because bank, tax and investment legislation varies from country to country, traffickers and their accomplices can find loopholes in national laws and procedures and can quickly adapt laundering schemes and techniques to hide their ill-gotten gains.

Suggested courses of action

At the national level

280.   Within the scope of the fundamental principles of the national legal systems, the legislature, ministries or other authorities concerned, university law faculties, research institutes and like academic bodies could review the national legislation and regulations and consider the desirability of proposing any necessary modifications that would facilitate and ensure the seizure, freezing, and forfeiture of the objects knowingly used in trafficking and the proceeds thereof, including objects knowingly acquired with those proceeds.

281.   The law could provide that, where it has been determined by appropriate judicial or administrative procedures that specific assets were acquired by means of the proceeds of trafficking, title to all such assets is forfeited. If some of these assets are located in another State, the State in which the action was initiated could assist that other State in seizing those assets.

282. States could in their legislation and regulations authorize their judicial or other authorities concerned to accede to appropriate requests for such actions from other States where the offence may have been committed.

283. Associations of banks, investment houses and like institutions should devise codes of conduct whereby their members would pledge themselves to assist the authorities in tracing the proceeds of trafficking activities. Subject to respect for the fundamental principles of national laws, the legislation could provide that the personnel and/or management of such firms will be liable to fines or other penalties if they knowingly participate in or facilitate schemes for concealing information relating to such transactions.

284. Subject to the limitations of the constitutional, legal and administrative system, the ministry concerned may wish to carry out, or cause to be carried out for the purpose of detecting the sources of illicit supply of drugs and of reducing that supply, an investigation into the income levels of persons suspected of serving as channels of supply. The investigators should be directed to look for evidence in the records of the tax authorities, motor vehicle licensing authorities, land registry, public register of companies and any other accessible statistical or financial records that may disclose a gap between declared income and ostentatious expenditure.

285. The ministry or other authority concerned should consider the desirability and possibility of establishing a special fund whose resources would be mobilized to serve the cause of the fight against the illicit drug traffic and drug abuse. The assets of the fund might be constituted from, for example, voluntary contributions, special governmental allocations, monies or property seized in connection with the prosecution and conviction of drug traffickers.

286. The distribution of the value of the proceeds of seizure and forfeiture could be a matter for agreement between the States concerned. Each State could empower an appropriate agency to establish a trust fund for holding such forfeited property.

At the regional and international levels

287. The Division of Narcotic Drugs in co-operation with ICPO/Interpol and CCC, assisted, as appropriate, by the United Nations Fund for Drug Abuse Control, should encourage the exchange of information about trans-border laundering schemes and techniques and of experience with the training of staff of law enforcement agencies and of financial institutions.

288. In cases where bilateral or multilateral agreements are negotiated for the purpose of promoting international trade, economic co-operation, cultural exchanges or for like purposes, the representatives of the States negotiating such agreements might consider the advisability of inserting in these instruments provisions designed to prevent legitimate transactions under the agreements from being used as vehicles for the laundering of gains from illicit drug trafficking, illicit drug manufacture and illicit cultivation of narcotic plants.

Target 24.   Tightening of controls of movement through official points of entry

The problem

289.   The security of airports, seaports and land border crossings is normally within the scope of responsibility of customs and, to a certain extent, immigration authorities. There are, however, usually gaps in the effective control by law enforcement agencies. For example, without full-time coverage, these entry points are vulnerable to penetration, as are other frontier areas. Even if covered on a full-time basis, the organization and layout of the facilities often offer opportunities for evasion of controls, and few entry points are equipped with modern or appropriate means of detecting illicit movements of drugs, such as sensing devices and sniffing dogs. Service personnel carrying out activities such as maintenance, cleaning, refuelling and catering, and crew members, are not always adequately controlled. Customs services are invariably under the jurisdiction of central government authorities, whereas the management of airports and seaports may be vested in a variety of local government or corporate entities. Organized private messenger and courier services moving across borders pose potential risks.

290.   The results obtained at the world level by law enforcement agencies responsible for combating illicit drug trafficking show that the largest seizures are now made in commercial freight, where drugs are concealed either among goods in normal traffic or inside specially fashioned cavities in means of transport. This form of carriage currently appears to be the preferred means of transportation of the highly organized trafficking networks. The expansion of international trade, the accelerated rotation of international means of transport and the development of containerized traffic should induce the supervising authorities to initiate action with respect to the establishment of effective national and international means of deterrence and enforcement which are compatible with a rapid flow of international trade.

Suggested courses of action

   At the national level

291.   Law enforcement agencies, customs services and the appropriate ministries or authorities could jointly analyse the current control systems, organization and layout of all official entry points with a view to recommending legislation and regulations or the redesign of facilities, in order to ensure full security control and appropriate jurisdictional authority over the physical facilities at all official entry points and so to curb illicit trafficking.

292.   Analogous measures might be taken with regard to the movement of goods into and out of free-trade zones or free ports, so that countries take the necessary steps to assure that free trade zones are not used to divert specific chemicals, precursors, and controlled drugs.

293.   While avoiding the restriction of or interference in international commerce, countries should develop programmes to ensure that all drugs or

chemicals entering or transiting their territory are of legitimate origin and destined for legitimate use. Countries should enact appropriate legislation for this purpose, where necessary. Appropriate law enforcement and customs officials should be trained in the identification of drugs and chemicals, suspicious routes and methods of illicit shipments. Manifests and shipping documents should be closely scrutinized for suspicious shipments. Authorities could be empowered to search incoming and outgoing vessels, aircraft and vehicles in order to monitor the movement and trans-shipment of drugs and chemicals in free trade areas. Patrols should be maintained in harbours, airports and other free zones.

294.   The appropriate law enforcement agency, usually the customs service, may initiate and implement these measures through the establishment of a joint task force with the agencies that manage the facilities of all official entry points and with the associations of transportation and shipping companies concerned.

295.   Appropriate training might be provided by the law enforcement agencies concerned to personnel involved in border controls. Such training could include techniques relating to the gathering and use of intelligence, the development of high-risk profiles and effective control of outward-bound passengers, particularly those departing for known drug source countries or regions.

296.   States might provide their appropriate law enforcement agencies with adequate sensing equipment, including trained dogs, and kits for the preliminary identification of suspect material; they might enlist the assistance of bilateral, multilateral or international agencies, if needed, for this purpose.

297.   The responsible authorities could seek, to the extent possible and by whatever means appear the most appropriate, to encourage shipping companies, rail and road transport undertakings and airlines serving international routes to enter into arrangements with the customs service, defining their respective responsibilities. Detailed arrangements may vary according to the degree of risk of drug trafficking and should whenever possible be based upon the Memoranda of Understanding established between CCC and the various international organizations concerned, e.g. the International Chamber of Shipping and the International Air Transport Association (IATA), and any accompanying guidelines detailing the co-operative measures to be taken by both the authorities and the members of those organizations. The law enforcement authority might undertake to provide training for the personnel in order to reduce these risks, while maintaining appropriate confidentiality.

298.   Within the scope of the fundamental principles of the national legal system, legislation could be enacted whereby firms whose employees are found to be in possession of large quantities of drugs acquired unlawfully in the course of their business would themselves be liable to penalties if proved to have been negligent in their management and to criminal penalties if their negligence rises to the level of recklessness.

299.   Notices and leaflets prominently displayed at embassies, consulates, airports, seaports and border crossings should warn travellers of the serious consequences of illegal trafficking and of the penal measures to which persons convicted of drug offences are liable.

300.   The appropriate ministry or authority could make regulations (in so far as they are not already in force) requiring industrial, manufacturing and trading corporations to report to the ministry or authority any case in which they have grounds for suspecting that goods, substances, equipment or any other item produced, manufactured or traded by them have been or are likely to be diverted to the illicit drug traffic or used for the purpose of making illicit drugs. In particular, the appropriate ministry or authority should instruct the licensing authority of the State, whether party to the 1961 and 1971 Conventions or not, to exercise caution in processing applications for export authorization for controlled drugs and should take steps to ensure the authenticity of the documents presented.

301.   The appropriate ministry or authority should issue instructions (if these do not already exist) to the customs service to verify the accuracy of the description given in the transport documents relating to suspect consignments of drugs entering or leaving the country and, in case of discrepancy or of misleading description, to refuse clearance of the goods in question, pending rectification bv the consignor.

At the regional and international levels

302.   The International Civil Aviation Organization (ICAO), the International Maritime Organization (IMO), the World Tourism Organization (WTO), IATA and the International Chamber of Shipping should consider and adopt (in so far as they have not already done so) standards or codes of conduct to be recommended to their members and designed to improve control of the movement of passengers and goods, with a view to curbing the illicit traffic in drugs. In this respect, and where they have not already done so, they should seek to establish memoranda of understanding with CCC.

303.   The United Nations Fund for Drug Abuse Control and regional and bilateral programmes should assist countries that need such assistance in equipping the law enforcement authorities at points of entry with drug sensing devices, trained sniffing dogs, drug identification kits and other means of control. The drug identification kit and related materials prepared by the Division of Narcotic Drugs can be made available in this connection.

304.   ICAO, IMO, the Universal Postal Union (UPU), WTO, ICPO/Interpol, CCC, IATA, the International Chamber of Shipping and the International Association of Ports and Harbors should provide, if requested, technical advice and assistance to Governments with respect to modalities for effecting appropriate physical security in standard layout and design of premises at official points of entry.

305.   Where a Government has reason to believe that its country is the target of an illicit supply of drugs originating in another country, it could consider entering into an agreement with the Government of that other country whereby it would be authorized to post duly qualified persons in that other country to co-operate with the local law enforcement agency in planning measures for stopping the supply.

Target 25. Strengthening of external border controls and of mutual assistance machinery within economic unions of sovereign States

The problem

306. Where a number of sovereign States have joined together to form an economic union or community by virtue of a treaty that provides, *inter alia,* for the free movement of goods and persons between the territories of its member States, it may be difficult or even impossible (because there are no intra-community border controls) to detect illicit movements of drugs and traffickers from one State to another.

Suggested courses of action

    At the national and regional levels

307. Without prejudice to the principle of freedom of movement of goods and persons laid down in the treaty establishing the union, the States members of the union would agree *inter se* to inform each other, and in particular the law enforcement agencies, of any suspect cross-border movement of drugs or of traffickers that comes to the notice of their authorities.

Target 26. Surveillance of land, water and air approaches to the frontier

The problem

308. Frontiers are particularly difficult to keep under effective surveillance and offer smugglers many opportunities for evasion. Similarly, in some countries possibilities for building private air strips and for effecting parachute deliveries in remote areas have been widely exploited by traffickers. To supplement the controls applied by the police and customs authorities at official points of entry, more complete coverage of frontiers, airspace and remote areas is needed to protect societies from the nefarious activities of the illicit traffickers in drugs.

Suggested courses of action

    At the national level

309. The forces which are responsible for or have jurisdiction over the controls at point of entry and other related agencies with responsibility in this area could develop, implement and, as appropriate, co-ordinate plans for the surveillance of air and water approaches by appropriate means and equipment in order that suspect movements may be reported promptly to customs and other law enforcement agencies. The coast guard or similar agencies could be authorized, on reasonable grounds of suspicion of illicit carriage of drugs, to stop and search vessels and aircraft within and over their territorial waters, without prejudice to the safety of such vessels and aircraft.

310.   The appropriate authorities should strictly enforce the existing domestic and international regulations regarding the registration of all aircraft—commercial or private—and enforce the obligation of all aircraft operators to operate strictly in accordance with approved flight plans and in conformity with the instructions of the air traffic control agencies.

311.   The appropriate ministry or authority could consider making regulations (where they do not already exist) requiring all privately owned boats, including pleasure craft, arriving from abroad outside any official port of entry, to report immediately to the nearest designated authority, giving full details of port of origin, cargo, passengers, owners and master of the ship or skipper, in order to request permission to refuel and obtain supplies. An aircraft entering or leaving the territory of the State should be strictly required to land at, or take off from, a designated customs airport (article 10 of the Convention on International Civil Aviation);[5] the appropriate authorities of each State have an internationally recognized right, without unreasonable delay, to search any aircraft on landing or departure, and to inspect the certificates and other documents prescribed by national law and/or by international conventions. The non-observance of such regulations would be punishable. Persons or companies providing fuel or supplies to such craft without verifying that they have permission would be liable to fines or other penalties.

312.   The appropriate ministry or authority should ensure that law enforcement agencies responsible for combating illicit trafficking are provided with efficient communication networks and means of transport and that their staff is trained to deal with drug trafficking between official points of entry. In countries that lack the financial resources to develop the necessary installations, networks, equipment and facilities for training, the Government might propose projects qualifying for multilateral or bilateral assistance or for assistance from UNFDAC for the purpose of obtaining them.

313.   Non-governmental associations of amateur pilots, yachtsmen and owners of pleasure craft and owners of private aircraft, boats and ferries, as well as associations of commercial and private fishermen and hunters and their individual members, are urged to co-operate with law enforcement authorities by reporting to these authorities suspected drug trafficking activities.

314.   Law enforcement agencies could consider the possibility of establishing telephone "hot lines" that are free of charge and connected to a permanently manned office, so that any person may report suspect drug-related occurrences without fear of reprisal.

315.   The appropriate ministry or authority could establish and maintain a system of licensing for private boats and marinas. The appropriate authorities should strictly enforce the existing domestic and international regulations concerning the registration of aircraft, the issuance of operator's permits and the use of properly designated airports or airstrips. Private operators and their organizations should be encouraged to report to law enforcement agencies suspected drug trafficking activity.

---

[5] *United Nations Treaty Series*, vol. 15, p. 295.

316.   The appropriate authorities could consider arranging for civic recognition or awards to individuals and non-governmental associations that have made outstanding contributions to the protection of the national frontiers against illicit drug trafficking.

At the regional and international levels

317.   The air traffic control agencies and other authorities concerned should strengthen flight control regulations in co-operation with their counterparts in the region and on a world-wide basis.

318.   The ministry or authority concerned, together with law enforcement agencies at the national and local levels, may wish to ensure that clear and effective channels of communication with corresponding agencies in other countries are established and maintained.

319.   Regional seminars should be organized to facilitate the exchange of ideas and techniques designed to strengthen frontier controls.

320.   The ministries or authorities concerned should take full advantage of regional and interregional co-operative mechanisms, of the sessions of the Commission on Narcotic Drugs and its Sub-Commission on Illicit Drug Traffic and Related Matters in the Near and Middle East, regional meetings of Heads of National Drug Law Enforcement Agencies, and of ICAO, IMO, CCC and ICPO/Interpol and IATA, in order to ensure maximum co-operation and consistency of implementation and training methods in safeguarding and strengthening the security of frontiers.

Target 27.   Controls over the use of the international mails for drug trafficking

The problem

321.   Customs services have determined by various techniques, including sniffing dogs, sensing devices, X-rays and the like, that controlled substances are being sent through the international mails notwithstanding the prohibition of such use of the post by the Universal Postal Convention. If the suspicious item is destined for delivery within the national territory, the customs service may obtain a search warrant and open the item for inspection, if the national laws so provide. However, if the suspicious item is in transit in the mails through the territory of the State whose authorities detect the illicit shipment, article 1 of the Universal Postal Convention and of the Constitution of UPU[6] provides that postal items in transit through a State party may not be opened. When this problem was discussed between CCC and UPU, the latter invited postal administrations:

   "(*a*)   To co-operate in combating the traffic in narcotics and psychotropic substances whenever they are legally required to do so by

---

[6]*United Nations Treaty Series*, vol. 611, Nos. 8844 and 8845, pp. 14 and 64.

their national authorities responsible for this matter; to ensure respect for the fundamental principles of the international post, in particular, the freedom of transit (article 1 of the Constitution and of the Convention);

"(*b*) To make all appropriate arrangements with the relevant authorities of their countries to ensure that bags of mail in transit suspected of enclosing items containing narcotics or psychotropic substances are not opened, but to:

"(i) Advise by the quickest means, at the request of their customs authorities, the administration of destination so that the suspected bags can easily be identified on arrival;

"(ii) Verify the origin of the mail."

In effect, this provides for a procedure not unlike controlled delivery for postal items in transit, a procedure already available with respect to items addressed to domestic destinations. However, the detection of suspicious items in the huge volumes of mail involved is no easy task, regardless of the destination of the items.

Suggested courses of action

At the national level

322. Within the scope of the constitutional order, the ministry responsible for postal communications and the national postal authorities could strengthen controls over the use of the international mails for drug trafficking. Items that are suspect by reason of origin, address, nature or other characteristics may be subjected to a test by a sensing device, sniffing dogs, X-ray or other mode of detection by postal authorities working closely with the appropriate law enforcement agency and:

(*a*) If the item is addressed to a person located in the national territory, the customs service should obtain a search warrant, if needed, and should inspect the item in accordance with domestic law and procedures;

(*b*) If the item is in postal transit, the customs service should urgently notify the customs authorities of the State of destination, by the quickest possible means, fully identifying the item and indicating its origin.

323. Local post offices could prominently display notices giving particulars of the penalties that are by law applicable to the use of the postal service for the carriage of controlled substances.

At the regional and international levels

324. UPU should provide States parties to the Universal Postal Convention with models of standard procedures for co-operation of postal authorities with customs.

325. The States parties to the Universal Postal Convention might further consider how to prevent the use of the international mails for drug trafficking;

for this purpose they may wish to propose appropriate amendments to the Convention. A study of this problem and of appropriate action which may be taken to combat it would be useful.

Target 28. Controls over ships on the high seas and aircraft in international airspace

The problem

326.   Vessels and aircraft are utilized for the illicit transport of drugs between countries, outside national boundaries, on the high seas and in international airspace. As numerous countries may be affected by the international shipment of drugs, appropriate co-operative procedures for interception need to be devised which do not interfere with legitimate passage and commerce, subject to compliance with existing relevant international conventions.

Suggested courses of action

  At the national level

327.   Should the ministry or authority concerned have reasonable grounds for suspecting that a vessel or aircraft registered under the laws of the State is illicitly carrying drugs, it may request another State to assist in carrying out a search: for example, that other State may be asked to direct its authorities to board and inspect the vessel and, if drugs are found, to seize them and arrest persons involved in the trafficking. In such circumstances, the State's own authorities may board or seize a vessel or aircraft registered under its laws.

328.   Subject to the provisions of international law, the law enforcement authorities should, to the fullest extent permitted by national law, undertake to board and seize a vessel unlawfully carrying drugs, provided that the authorization of the State of registry and, when applicable, of a coastal State has been obtained. A State should endeavour to respond promptly when asked for permission to stop, board and search a vessel under its registry for reasons of illicit drug trafficking control. Subject to the same considerations, an aircraft may be subject to search upon landing at a designated airport.

329.   The appropriate ministry or authority should, after the seizure of such a vessel or aircraft, deal promptly with illicit drugs and traffickers found thereon under the country's own laws if the conveyance is registered under that country's laws or, if registered under the laws of another State, pursuant to such agreement as is reached with the State of registry without unnecessary delay.

330.   States could authorize the appropriate agency or responsible authority to take appropriate action in these matters. This action might include the prompt communication of information indicating whether a particular vessel or aircraft is registered under the laws of the requested State and also authority to empower a requesting State to seize the suspect vessel or aircraft.

At the regional and international levels

331. International bodies and States could consider whether international standards can be established for the identification, seizure and disposition of vessels and aircraft on the surface suspected of carrying drugs illicitly, and of the drugs and traffickers found thereon. States should also make every effort to conclude bilateral, multilateral and regional agreements to strengthen such co-operation between States.

332. Existing intergovernmental forums, including the transport and shipping programmes of the regional commissions, should consider the question of illicit drug movement, the need to co-ordinate efforts to halt it, and the importance of support for the new convention.

Chapter IV

TREATMENT AND REHABILITATION

Introduction

333.   In many cultural patterns and in many regions, man has had recourse to drugs for various purposes: ritualistic, initiatory, diagnostic, dionysiac or therapeutic. In response to the obvious dangers, societies have made laws or pronounced taboos to prevent abuse and to protect the community.

334.   The upsurge of drug addiction since the 1960s represents a previously unknown phenomenon, at least so far as its dimensions are concerned. Addiction has spread over the entire planet, sparing almost no nation, no social class and no age, regardless of sex and race. The damage caused to the physical, psychological and social health of individuals and of communities has made drug addiction a public hazard on the world scale. Addiction has become a matter of serious concern to many Governments, for it affects public and social health and economic resources. In some countries, drug abuse is regarded as an offence and persons are prosecuted for drug abuse and are liable to penalties. Moreover, the stigma attached to drug addiction may lead to a reluctance to apply for assistance and treatment at available services.

335.   Because drug addiction is a phenomenon with world dimensions and ramifications, the treatment and rehabilitation of addicts call for collaboration on a global scale and in a multidisciplinary context at the national, regional and international levels.

336.   Development of a policy for treatment for drug addiction is difficult and complex, because it must include counselling, guidance, motivation, treatment in the medical sense, rehabilitation and social reintegration and should ideally culminate in the drug addict's return to a drug-free life. Great importance should be ascribed to social, cultural and environmental factors. Particular stress is laid on the multidisciplinary aspects of the strategy of treatment and rehabilitation, which involves the participation of a wide range of experts from several specialities. Account must be taken of the establishment and maintenance of parent/family and peer groups designed to support the drug addict throughout the treatment and aftercare process. These psycho-social support structures can greatly enhance the potential for recovery and prevention of relapse. In fact, a successful treatment mitigates the health and social consequences of drug abuse and thus reduces *pari passu* the use of drugs, the activities of traffickers and the risks of relapse. A high degree of commitment on the part of the addict plays a crucial role.

73

337. Developing countries have particular problems where drug addiction becomes an additonal burden on limited resources. Special attention should be given to the needs of developing countries and ways in which approaches to treatment and rehabilitation can be developed which take account of the economic, cultural and social constraints upon these countries.

Target 29. Towards a policy of treatment

The problem

338. The definition of a clear and precise policy is fundamental to the conduct of treatment operations. It is well known that, apart from its health and social implications, drug abuse has economic repercussions which constitute serious handicaps to the development of some countries, impairing the productivity of citizens and representing heavy charges on medical and social support systems. Treatment has often suffered from the lack of guiding principles and a lack of cohesion—each category of experts tended to pursue its own programme in isolation. For a long time, law enforcement measures played, directly or indirectly, an important part as the only alternative to treatment. Owing to the inconsistency of the results of this combination with those obtained by self-help associations, for example, the concept that eventually prevailed was that drug addiction was a disease amenable to treatment. For this purpose, a coherent policy of action is needed, avoiding dissipation or duplication of effort and making possible the integration of the programme into the general primary health care plan. It must be a policy that permits the judicious choice of objectives, the identification of target groups at risk and the establishment of an order of priorities. Therapeutic measures can operate more effectively with the participation of the community and when such measures ensure that the addict remains within the context of the community.

Suggested courses of action

At the national level

339. The competent national authorities concerned, where appropriate, in collaboration with non-governmental organizations, may consider establishing a nation-wide co-ordinating body to be responsible for co-ordinating and giving guidance to the development and maintenance of a comprehensive national treatment programme for drug addiction.

340. It is essential to collect data without prejudice to confidentiality, and then to identify priority targets and groups at risk and to estimate the cost of programmes and the resources available. The medical files of health services, the records of the social service and court documents are all potential sources of data. The data should be supplemented by systematic field surveys, which might be carried out by researchers and institutes in the social sciences.

341.   The ministry or authority concerned with health matters, in conjunction with the ministries or authorities responsible for education, law enforcement, security, employment etc., could work out, in the light of the data gathered by statistical services, customs authorities or other agencies concerning drug abuse, illicit trafficking and the incidence of drug-related diseases such as acquired immune deficiency syndrome (AIDS) and hepatitis, a national policy, and a programme for its implementation, for preventing and reducing drug addiction and for reintegrating drug addicts into social and occupational life. The national policy and the implementation programme might, as appropriate, pay attention to intravenous drug abuse and to countering the spread of HIV virus among this group of drug abusers. Provision should be made for the periodic testing of the functioning of the programme.

342.   The various targets, methods and priorities should be strictly laid down in order to facilitate implementation of the programme. Work should proceed on the basis of and with the facilities available, improvements being introduced progressively. The start should not be delayed by aspirations to achieve perfection and the programme should not be limited to an "all-or-nothing" approach. Methods which do not take account of the actual local situation should be avoided. Allowance should be made for the changing nature of addiction by making provision for possible adjustments in the light of the demands of the moment.

343.   Incentives could be offered to bodies and institutions in the private sector which carry on research into drug abuse or which perform therapeutic functions, social welfare services or services of some other kind in support of the community efforts to combat drug abuse and to treat drug addicts.

At the international level

344.   WHO should indicate the principal factors to be taken into account in the formulation of a policy for the treatment of drug addiction.

345.   United Nations organizations, including in particular the regional commissions, which undertake activities in the various aspects of social development should incorporate issues related to the treatment and rehabilitation of drug abusers into their social development programmes.

346.   Member States should involve WHO in establishing or strengthening national policy for the treatment of drug addiction.

347.   WHO should be urged to prepare, in co-operation with international and governmental organizations, a plan for disseminating knowledge about the way in which national treatment policies can be established and strengthened.

348.   The work of WHO on nosology should be encouraged and expanded, and governments should assist WHO in field testing the validity of the nosology in various locations.

Target 30. Inventory of available modalities and techniques
of treatment and rehabilitation

The problem

349. After an action policy has been adopted, an inventory is needed of the modalities and techniques actually available at the national level for undertaking the treatment, rehabilitation and social reintegration of drug addicts. In most countries, many different services and agencies are involved in the prevention of drug abuse and in the treatment and rehabilitation of drug abusers. Some are specialist, others are generalist. Some are centrally funded, others locally funded, and some depend on voluntary contributions. In the absence of evaluation and co-ordination this network of services will develop haphazardly and without regard to the manner in which each is expected to complement the others.

350. It is important that the treatment system should be carefully planned and properly co-ordinated in order to make better use of existing resources. Appropriate intervention, possibilities for care and referral mechanisms should be available and be integrated within the primary health care system. Furthermore, it is essential that the provision of services in all of the treatment areas should be monitored and evaluated. Sound monitoring and evaluation can lead to efficient and cost-effective use of resources.

Suggested courses of action

At the national level

351. The appropriate authority could:

(*a*) Draw up an inventory of and evaluate the facilities for treatment actually available at the national level, their capacities and their locations. The inventory should include information regarding the staffing, objectives, methods and other characteristics of the treatment provided at the primary care community level, and as specialist health and social services;

(*b*) In co-operation with the fiscal, legislative and other appropriate authorities, adjust the apportionment of resources in the light of priority targets and of the groups at risk;

(*c*) Evaluate the material and manpower in the various professional categories involved, taking into account the resources actually available at the national level.

(*d*) Evaluate the effectiveness of treatment approaches making use of WHO advice on treatment outcome evaluation.

352. The appropriate authority could evaluate the efficacy of methods of dealing with cases of drug abuse or, in cases where it considers that other, more effective methods could be applied, may recommend a change of methods. From time to time it could critically evaluate the progress made and make recommendations for the future. The persons in charge of the treatment and rehabilitation centres should participate in the evaluation process.

At the regional and international levels

353. Close collaboration should be established or maintained with international organizations (especially with WHO) and with non-governmental organizations so that information on treatment approaches and outcomes can be adapted to specific local and national settings. In the light of this information, national strategies may, as appropriate, be revised.

354. WHO, in collaboration with the Division of Narcotic Drugs, regional organizations and international non-governmental organizations, should gather data on modalities and techniques of treatment available, as well as on their application. Such information should be widely disseminated by WHO, in particular to countries that lack relevant experience.

355. Exchanges of experts with other countries should be encouraged under the auspices of WHO. These exchanges should make it possible to form a comparative and objective estimate of the progress of work.

356. International organizations should provide technical assistance as requested to evaluate the efficacy of national programmes of treatment. WHO, in co-operation with Governments, should consider developing comparable evaluation design and methodology for treatment outcome studies. International organizations should assist in disseminating the findings and in comparing results.

357. International organizations (including UNFDAC, WHO and ILO), non-governmental organizations and Governments should be requested to provide technical assistance and, if needed, financial assistance, for epidemiological studies, including research to identify high risk groups and to establish the aetiology of drug addiction.

358. At the request of Governments or intergovernmental organizations, regional seminars on available modalities and techniques of treatment and rehabilitation could be organized for more extensive information and mutual benefit. Experts from ILO, WHO, UNESCO and other bodies whose experience in their respective fields is essential could participate in these seminars. Assistance by the United Nations Fund for Drug Abuse Control may be required.

359. Regional training and retraining courses could be arranged, enabling participants to learn about the latest developments in the field of the treatment of drug addiction, rehabilitation and re-integration of drug addicts.

360. The need for a common language calls for the preparation by WHO of a glossary of terms and expressions in use in the area of drug addiction. With the aid of such a glossary, experts of various nationalities would be able to understand each other better and more accurately. These terms should be defined operationally and tested for validity before dissemination with the necessary consideration of medical, social and legal connotations, including the provisions of international law.

361. A handbook or compendium of treatment and rehabilitation techniques prepared by WHO, in collaboration with ILO, for use by workers in the field would be of great value. The available manuals on treatment techniques should be reviewed and, if appropriate, revised as necessary for broad applicability and after field testing made readily available.

Target 31. Selection of appropriate treatment programmes

The problem

362. The selection of treatment programmes is fraught with various difficulties. It should take account of the local social, cultural and environmental factors for the purpose of mobilizing local resources and energies and facilitating a drug addict's social reintegration. The programme model should be personalized, i.e. its thrust and form should correspond to the nature of the drug and to the personality of the drug abuser. Drugs do not all produce the same kinds of addiction. Some people misuse drugs without being addicted. Also, people who have recourse to drugs do so for different reasons. In some cases the use of drugs masks a pathological condition.

363. Such techniques as continued provision of controlled amounts of addictive substances have not been universally accepted. However, some countries consider that programmes in which substitutes are prescribed are appropriate in reducing illicit drug use. Other modalities of treatment or drug-free therapeutic communities are successful in reducing the rate of recidivism.

364. Detoxification represents only a part of the treatment and rehabilitation process. Detoxification must therefore be succeeded by rehabilitation, which is a long process aimed at teaching the individual to resume civic life free of the chains of the drug. The rehabilitated drug abuser learns to give a meaning to life, to establish a healthy relationship with others and to face the difficulties of day-to-day life without recourse to drugs.

Suggested courses of action

  At the national level

365. With respect to the technique and course of treatment, a national or regional optimum therapeutic programme should be elaborated in the light of the different conditions of the countries or regions concerned. Scientific research should be strengthened in order to guide the clinical practice of primary health care agencies. WHO and other international organizations can sum up the experience of various countries and promote the exchange of information.

366. The appropriate ministry or authority could issue guidelines addressed to the members of the medical and paramedical professions and to educational establishments, social welfare agencies and others concerned, recommending

that, in cases where they have to deal with drug addicts, they should not ignore the possibility that the addiction or abuse had its origin in a psychopathological or psycho-social condition, which may require treatment by psychotherapeutic or chemo-therapeutical means.

367.   The ministry or authority concerned could issue guidelines recommending that those administering treatment should adjust the mode of treatment in the light of changing patterns of drug use, e.g. the appearance of more potent drugs, increased poly-drug use, and other factors. In addition, they should take into account situations where the drug habit is aggravated or complicated by psycho-social factors, or by the presence of certain diseases, or other conditions, such as pregnancy.

368.   The appropriate ministry or authority, in countries where drug addiction has assumed or threatens to assume serious dimensions, could establish centres (in so far as they do not already exist) for carrying out detoxification operations and for treating serious cases. The availability and possible success of treatment should be made known to the public. Provision should be made for seeking out drug addicts in their customary environment with a view to guiding them towards treatment; this function might be fulfilled by social workers.

369.   Where appropriate, it might be desirable to enlist the participation of groups of volunteers and former addicts, subject to appropriate training and satisfactory evidence of their qualifications in the treatment and rehabilitation teams.

370.   Treatment programmes should make provision for involving the families of drug addicts. In countries where the resident population is covered by public health insurance schemes it might be useful for the various ministries concerned (e.g. health, finance, social welfare, labour) to obtain precise information on the cost to the nation, for example in terms of public funds, time lost, personnel, material and medicaments, of the treatment of drug addicts that necessitates their absence from school or training courses or from work. In the light of the information and of the success rate of treatment the ministry concerned may make recommendations concerning the circumstances in which out-patient treatment of such persons may be preferable to their in-patient treatment.

371.   Where appropriate, the ministry concerned may wish to recommend that health insurance schemes, whether public or private, should offer the insured persons coverage of the expenses of detoxification, treatment for drug abuse and rehabilitation.

372.   The persons in charge of assistance centres should be able to carry out "individualized" treatment programmes geared to the drug addict's genuine problems and should involve, as appropriate, the person's family; the treatment should, if necessary, deal with drug-related diseases and include pharmacological or psychotherapeutic treatment, social assistance, participation in a community, etc. The treatment should be chosen on the basis of the best possible diagnosis and of an evaluation of its true efficacy, as well as on the basis of a cost-benefit evaluation.

373.   In urban environments where the risk of addiction is considered to be particularly high in certain social groups or age groups, the civic or municipal authority might be invited by the ministry concerned to establish a permanently staffed emergency aid centre specially designed to respond to urgent appeals for help by addicts or their families.

374.   The ministry concerned, taking account of the national legislation, might consider the possibility of supporting private initiatives such as self-help associations which have proved to be useful in providing care for drug abusers or for persons at risk of becoming drug addicts or for persons who have undergone a course of treatment for addiction and who may need to be protected against relapse. Such initiatives may relieve congestion in public health institutions and may be found to be cost-effective.

At the regional and international levels

375.   WHO may be asked by Governments to send experts to help in setting up a treatment programme.

376.   Regional meetings should be organized by regional bodies to assess the progress of work and consider future projects regarding the treatment of drug addiction. The United Nations regional commissions could provide an appropriate forum for such meetings, organized in collaboration with WHO.

377.   International organizations (in particular WHO and ILO) and other appropriate organizations as well as non-governmental organizations should review existing operational manuals available for sponsors of treatment programmes, determine if a need exists for additional or improved manuals, and, if so, revise or prepare them as necessary and distribute them.

378.   The appropriate authorities or ministries concerned with treatment and rehabilitation should consider the possibility of seconding to each other senior staff in charge of treatment programmes, in order that they may have an opportunity to broaden their experience.

Target 32.   Training for personnel working with drug addicts

The problem

379.   Social service and health personnel who deal with drug addicts have undergone a basic university or university-type education designed to provide them with the fundamental technical skills and specific knowledge needed for the performance of their professional activities. This basic training must, however, be supplemented by specific training programmes to enable them to develop their aptitude for an activity that is essentially interdisciplinary, for treatment can only be effective if it takes into account both the medical and psychological problems of the addict and those that are sociological in nature and related to the surroundings.

380. In view of the fact that numerous other professionals and officials come into contact with addicts, these persons should be provided with appropriate training regarding not only the cultural aspects of drug addiction, but also the treatment centres whose services are available to them in cases of need.

Suggested courses of action

At the national level

381. The appropriate authority might consider appointing working groups consisting of experts, specialist workers and other competent people working closely with cases of drug abuse to design specific curricula and training courses for specific groups of professionals, volunteers and community leaders.

382. Where provision for training already exists, the working group should identify and fill gaps in the curriculum. This should be done through close consultation with persons and organizations responsible for the delivery of services. The curriculum for personnel working with drug addicts should contain a syllabus concerning the treatment, management, and rehabilitation of drug dependent persons.

383. Specialized training courses should be established (in so far as they do not already exist) that confer professional and academic status (i.e. recognized by professional bodies or teaching institutions) and degrees or titles entitling graduates of the course to certain advantages (e.g. seniority or higher salary). Wherever possible, training courses should be multidisciplinary bringing together all workers concerned with similar issues, including lawyers, judges and prison officers, teachers and community workers.

384. Professional organizations could include rules of conduct concerning the handling of drug-related cases in their general rules or professional standards.

At the international level

385. Specialized agencies, other international organizations and non-governmental organizations should, on request, provide advice on the content of existing training courses and suggest general guidelines for States wishing to establish courses *de novo*.

386. In addition, these organizations should review existing materials available for training purposes, revise the material if necessary and make it available for integration within national training programmes for application by local training staff.

387. Training projects conducted by United Nations organizations, especially the regional commissions, related to social development, primary health care and special population groups should have a training and rehabilitation component which utilizes WHO material and which reports to WHO the responses to this training and its use.

388. In certain parts of the world it may be cost-effective to establish courses on a regional rather than a national basis. The regional offices of WHO may be consulted in cases where countries wish to initiate regional training courses concentrating on the treatment of drug addiction.

Target 33. Reduction of the incidence of diseases and the number of infections transmitted through drug-using habits

The problem

389. A large number of persons misusing drugs suffer from diseases not caused by the drug itself but by secondary factors connected with a certain life style or a special method of drug application (especially intravenous), thus creating health hazards not only to themselves but also to others. While some of those hazards may affect individuals only (e.g. damage to the column of the nose caused by sniffing habits), others may have a wider impact, such as AIDS and certain communicable diseases, such as hepatitis, which may be spread by the use of the same hypodermic syringe by different persons, one of whom has the disease. The adverse health consequences of drug abuse and addiction on the next generation are only partially known. The study of the short- and long-term damage of drug taking to future generations has to be intensified.

Suggested courses of action

At the national level

390. The ministry or authority concerned with public health might collect the data available on the frequency of contagious diseases among drug users. For this purpose the ministry or authority might undertake or cause to be carried out (in so far it has not already done so) a scientific investigation to determine, *inter alia*:

(*a*) The different diseases prevalent among the drug-using population, the number of persons already infected and the number of persons at risk;

(*b*) The channels of contagion and their possible relation to the drug-using habit;

(*c*) Possible means of halting the transmission of disease.

391. Especially in cases where possible infections tend to become a health hazard to larger segments of the society and where a certain drug-using habit cannot be stopped immediately but is known to accelerate the spread of the contagion, the ministry or authority concerned with public health should consider inviting experts to study possible prophylactic measures which will not promote or facilitate drug abuse and to make recommendations accordingly. The ministry or authority and other appropriate agencies could publish information about those health hazards and about ways of avoiding them, both among the drug-using population and in the community at large. The ministry

or authority and other appropriate agencies could also consider expanding treatment capacity and incorporating treatment outreach programmes for intravenous drug users as a means of interrupting the transmission of disease.

At the international level

392.   Information about experience in the field of the treatment of drug-related infectious diseases should be communicated to WHO, which should analyse the data and publish its conclusions.

393.   WHO may be asked by the ministry or authority concerned with public health to send experts or provide other information about such diseases to help to identify existing health hazards, groups at risk and possible dangers in the future and in planning strategies for counteracting them.

394.   WHO should consider publishing guidelines addressed to a broad range of professionals and authorities as well as family members for dealing with drug use in cases where drug use is associated with contagious diseases. WHO should be requested to study this problem.

395.   The scientific community at large and drug manufacturers should continue their efforts to invent and develop vaccines, medicines and other remedies to prevent and cure AIDS and other drug-abuse related infectious diseases.

Target 34.   Care for drug-addicted offenders within the criminal justice and prison system

The problem

396.   According to the provisions of the 1961 Convention [article 36, paragraph 1(*b*) and article 38, paragraph 1] and the 1971 Convention [article 20, paragraph 1, and article 22, paragraph 1(*b*)] the parties should consider providing, either as an alternative to conviction or punishment or in addition to punishment, that abusers of drugs and/or of psychotropic substances should undergo measures of treatment, education, after-care, rehabilitation and social reintegration.

397.   A large number of drug-abusing persons come into contact with the criminal justice system. In some States drug-related offences represent more than half of all the criminal cases dealt with by the courts. As a consequence, many of the offenders are then channelled through the correctional institutions, and in some States offenders convicted of drug-related offences form the majority of the prison population.

398.   Hence the criminal justice and correctional system occupies a prominent place in the handling, treatment and rehabilitation of persons who have committed a criminal offence against the legislation governing narcotic drugs and psychotropic substances or a criminal offence for the purpose of obtaining illicit supplies thereof or while under the influence of such drugs or substances.

Suggested courses of action

At the national level

399. The appropriate ministry or authority, in collaboration with the other ministries or authorities concerned, could collect the data available on the incidence of drug addiction among offenders. The ministry or authority might take appropriate actions to ensure that effective care and treatment are provided to offenders who are drug addicts.

400. In countries where it is known or believed that a substantial proportion of the total prison population is accounted for by persons serving sentences imposed for drug-related offences, or being held in custody pending trial for an alleged drug-related offence, the ministry concerned could undertake or cause to be carried out (in so far as it has not already done so) a scientific investigation, conducted with due regard to preserving anonymity, for the purpose of determining, *inter alia*:

(*a*) The number of persons serving sentences for offences involving drugs or drug-related offences, broken down according to age groups;

(*b*) The number of persons in custody charged with such an offence and awaiting trial;

(*c*) The proportion of the total prison population accounted for by persons convicted of or charged with drug-related offences, including offences committed by drug addicts;

(*d*) The type and number of offences committed by persons in the categories described in the preceding subparagraphs;

(*e*) The male-female ratio among prisoners convicted of or charged with drug-related offences;

(*f*) The proportion among prisoners convicted of or charged with such offences that is accounted for by persons previously convicted or accused of such an offence;

(*g*) The proportion of such prisoners that is accounted for by persons who have previously received therapeutic treatment by reason of drug addiction.

401. In the light of the results of the investigation, the ministry or ministries concerned could consider in what respects the national plan or policy for dealing with drug abuse and illicit trafficking needs to be reviewed, amended or strengthened with a view to reducing the number of persons imprisoned by reason of drug-related offences. If it should decide to publish a report containing the results of the investigation, the ministry could invite research institutes, research workers, sociologists, criminologists, experts in the law, specialized non-governmental organizations and other interested bodies to submit comments on the report and to suggest remedial measures.

402. In countries where the relevant information is not yet available and where the treatment of drug addiction is under study or review, the ministry or authority concerned with public health might consider carrying out or causing

to be carried out a statistical survey for the purpose of determining what proportion of the inmates of penal, correctional and other closed institutions is accounted for by drug abusers and former drug addicts. In the light of the data and after consultation with experts, the ministry or authority may wish to make appropriate changes—if needed—in the national policy for the treatment of drug addiction, or in the guidelines for the treatment of drug addicts, or in the conditions governing admission to and discharge from such institutions.

403. In cases where the appropriate national authority is contemplating preparing new legislation that would make drug-related offences punishable by more severe penalties than are applicable in respect of such offences under the existing law, it could invite comments on its proposals from scholars and experts in the law, from youth leaders, social workers and others having direct experience of the behaviour of drug addicted offenders. The principal object of such consultations would be to ensure that the proposed legislation will not conflict with the longer-term objectives of the campaign for reducing the illicit demand for drugs, drug abuse and illicit trafficking and will not tend to add to the number of hardened offenders.

404. The appropriate authority might direct (in so far as it has not already done so) that the necessary medical, educational and support care should be provided for drug addicts held in custody pending trial and for convicted drug abusers.

At the international level

405. The Centre for Social Development and Humanitarian Affairs of the United Nations Office at Vienna should co-ordinate, in co-operation with the United Nations Social Defence Research Institute, the United Nations regional institutes for crime prevention and control and WHO, research into the interdependence of activities for the prevention of crime and the treatment of offenders.

406. The ministries concerned could arrange exchanges of experience of treatment alternatives and intramural rehabilitation efforts, especially for staff of the judicial system and personnel of the correctional system.

407. WHO and the United Nations Social Defence Research Institute might consider preparing guidelines for the treatment of drug offenders who are drug addicts.

Target 35. Social reintegration of persons who have undergone programmes for treatment and rehabilitation

The problem

408. A former drug abuser is a fragile being who has passed through a difficult stage. Assistance is needed by such persons in order that they should

be able to readjust to social life and its constraints. By helping the individual to take a place in its midst, society is helping itself. The community, which, after all, has stood by the drug addict throughout the period of treatment, should mobilize resources for assisting this person thereafter. Drug addiction should be viewed as a chronic recurring disorder which responds to treatment. Several treatment episodes may be necessary before long-term abstinence is realized. The treatment of a drug addict does not end until the addict is reintegrated into society.

409.   In most cases, drug addiction occurs first at an age when the person has not yet acquired mastery of a trade or occupation, or else, if addiction occurs later, it often disorganizes work habits. The adult drug addict who has been treated runs into almost insurmountable difficulties in attempting to resume civic life. Hence, vocational and social rehabilitation techniques could be employed to assist reintegration of addicts into society.

410.   Promoting social rehabilitation is an important part of the aid process because both during and after treatment addicts and former addicts often have no realistic prospects in society in the sense of training opportunities and accommodation. The necessary attention should therefore be given at the earliest possible stage to developing genuine social alternatives for drug addicts. This means that such matters as housing (supervised or otherwise), vocational training and appropriate work, training for work and assistance in finding employment are not only important in the after-care stage but also constitute an inseparable element of treatment, to be incorporated from the outset. Only then can addicts be sufficiently motivated to take part in an aid programme.

411.   The purpose of treatment is to secure the individual's return to a drug-free life. This is rendered difficult by a series of factors for which allowance must be made: the prejudices that in some social groups stain the reputation of the drug abuser, even after treatment, poor or non-existent occupational qualifications, awkwardness and poor performance at school and at work, resistance to discipline, tendency to instability—all these are negative factors on the road back to a productive drug-free social life. Moreover, some former drug addicts, for fear of revealing their past, are reluctant to offer themselves openly on the labour market; they do not dare to make use of the social niches placed by society at the disposal of all.

412.   The guiding principle is that the particular programme should be adopted which is most cost-effective within the community. Attention should be given to on-the-job apprenticeships in various crafts. Master craftsmen in the community may accept apprentices in return for some financial compensation by the community. This policy is sometimes preferable to the establishment of vocational centres or schools, which calls for the investment of resources not always immediately available, particularly in the developing countries.

413.   In appropriate settings, consideration might be given to the rehabilitative value of outdoor work for addicts. In the rural environment vocational training might concentrate on agricultural pursuits.

Suggested courses of action

At the national level

414. Inasmuch as the success of treatment and rehabilitation of drug addicts can be evaluated by reference to the extent to which the harm caused by drug abuse has been reduced, as well as by reference to the extent to which they have been integrated into society and into a drug-free environment at home as well as at work, and as the risk of recidivism is always present where the facilities and resources for after-care are lacking or inadequate, the appropriate authority could ensure that after-care services, including the assistance of social workers, are provided on a scale commensurate with needs. Also treatment and rehabilitation programmes could include follow-up programmes.

415. In order to prevent a relapse after the return of the ex-addict to his previous environment, the ministry or authority concerned with public health or social welfare could consider establishing "transit" institutions in which the ex-addict could be trained, through work and education, to an appropriate life-style, in a therapeutic environment.

416. Youth movements, sports clubs and like associations, as well as associations of former drug users, should be encouraged to make their contribution towards the rehabilitation and social reintegration of former drug users.

417. In appropriate cases religious organizations might provide assistance to former drug users. Where these exist, ministries of religious affairs might wish to issue guidelines for religious groups to take part in the effort of treatment and rehabilitation.

418. The ministry or authority concerned with education, in conjunction with other ministries or authorities concerned and voluntary bodies (e.g. parent organizations), could initiate or expand programmes for associating families in the process of rehabilitation and reintegration.

419. By reason of the deleterious effect of enforced idleness, particularly among the young, the ministry or other authority concerned with employment might take into account, when shaping the country's employment policy, the desirability of introducing a wider range of occupational training and creating employment opportunities for persons specially vulnerable to the risks of drug abuse, because of their age, social environment, lack of skills or for any other reason. The ministry concerned could consider working out, in consultation with employers' and workers' organizations, special training (including on-the-job training) for the benefit of such persons, and if possible should support such schemes by the grant of financial or other assistance.

420. The ministry or authority concerned with public health could give strict instructions, applicable to both public and private institutions, clinics, hospitals or other treatment centres, to the effect that confidential data disclosed to the centre or institution concerned by a medical practitioner about drug users who have received or are under treatment there, or disclosed by the persons themselves, must not be divulged to any unauthorized person or agency and

must not in any case be used in any manner that might prejudice their chances of resuming a position in society and of finding employment.

421.   Employers should be invited to contribute to the treatment of addicted employees by keeping the workplace open during the period of treatment or agreeing to the person's reinstatement after discharge. At enterprise level, early detection and assistance under conditions of confidentiality should be encouraged.

422.   The ministry or authority concerned with employment questions could urge employers, as part of the rehabilitation process, to provide equal employment opportunities to former drug addicts.

423.   Trade union organizations should consider assisting the family of any member who has become addicted and who is under treatment.

424.   The support of professional and occupational associations and chambers of commerce and industry should be enlisted for the purpose of opening up possibilities of apprenticeship and placement for former addicts. Social workers should help in finding employment for such persons.

425.   The ministry or authority concerned might wish to consider inviting a non-governmental organization to suggest a scheme for aiding persons who have been receiving treatment for drug addiction and who have good prospects of being cured to readjust to life in society. Such a scheme might be modelled *mutatis mutandis* on those operated by discharged prisoners' aid societies, and should avoid any hint of moral stigma attaching to the person concerned. Similarly, the ministry or authority concerned might consider inviting philanthropic or other non-governmental organizations to offer aid and counselling services to former drug abusers and their families in need of advice or support.

At the regional and international levels

426.   Governments and workers' and employers' organizations may wish to ask ILO for technical assistance and expert advice in setting up schemes for the reintegration of former drug addicts in occupational activities or for their vocational training or retraining. ILO might consider publishing guidelines for this purpose, as well as arranging for exchanges of experience with respect to methods of reintegrating drug addicts into society.

427.   Regional bodies, including non-governmental organizations, might consider establishing schemes to be operated jointly by two or more of their member countries for the social reintegration of former drug addicts.

INDEX

A. Keywords of the Comprehensive Multidisciplinary Outline of Future Activities in Drug Abuse Control

Keyword	*Paragraph, chapter (target)*
1961 Single Convention	2,6,15,16,17 Introduction, 18 I(Introduction), 55 I(2), 123,124 II(Introduction), 128 II(8), 173,176 II(12), 188,189 II(14), 204,206 II(15), 233 III(17), 253 III(19), 271 III(22), 278 III(23), 300 III(24), 396 IV(34)
1971 Convention	2,6,15,16,17 Introduction, 18 I(Introduction), 127 II(Introduction), 158,159,161,162 II(10), 166,170,172 II(11), 173,176 II(12), 206 II(15), 233 III(17), 253 III(19), 271 III(22), 278 III(23), 300 III(24), 396 IV(34)
1972 Protocol	2,6,16,17 Introduction, 123 II(Introduction)
academic (institutions)	12,14 Introduction, 32 I(1), 129,131 II(8), 146,151 II(9), 272 III(22), 280 III(23),
acquired immune deficiency syndrome (AIDS)	341 IV(29)
administrative control	6,8 Introduction
advertisement	146,154 II(9)
aerial survey	197 II(14)
aetiology	15 Introduction, 50 I(2), 357 IV(30)
aftercare	88 I(5), 336 IV(Introduction)
aggravating circumstances	274 III(22)
aircraft	201 II(15), 293 III(24), 309,310,311,313,315 III(26), Title,326,327,328,329,330,331 III(28)
airport	231 III(17), 289,293,299 III(24), 311,315 III(26), 328 III(28)
alcohol	17 Introduction, 75 I(4)
analogue	Title,181,182,183,184,185,186,187 II(13)
arms	223 III(Introduction), 241 III(17), 274 III(22)
availability of drugs	6 Introduction, 225 III(Introduction)

Keyword	Paragraph, chapter (target)
bank	223 III(Introduction), 231,238 III(17), 279,283 III(23)
bank secrecy	257,260 III(20)
border control	295 III(24), Title,306 III(25)
cannabis	125 II(Introduction), 188,191,192 II(14), 199,204,206 II(15), 217,219 II(16)
cash crops	195 II(14), 210,211 II(16)
causes (of drug abuse)	5 Introduction, 23 I(Introduction), 33,41 I(1), 48 I(2), 57,72 I(3)
chemo-therapeutical (treatment)	366 IV(31)
civic (organizations)	Title,88,89,93 I(5), 409 IV(35)
co-ordinating (agency, body, machinery)	15 Introduction, 29 I(1), 68 I(3), 94 I(5), 206 II(15), 233 III(17), 339 IV(29)
coast guard	309 III(26)
coca bush	125,126 II(Introduction), 188,189,191,192 II(14), 206 II(15), 219 II(16)
coca-leaf	126 II(Introduction)
coca-leaf chewing	126 II(Introduction)
cocaine	126 II(Introduction)
community (organizations, activities)	15 Introduction, 29 I(1), 58,63 I(3), 74 I(4), Title,85,86,87,89,90,91,92,93,96 I(5), 97,99,101 I(6), 110,112 I(7), 338,343 IV(29), 351 IV(30), 372 IV(31), 381,383 IV(32), 408 IV(35)
comparative studies	34 I(1), 137 II(8)
conditional release	271,275 III(22)
confidentiality	43 I(2), 234 III(17), 297 III(24), 340 IV(29), 421 IV(35)
conspiracy	223 III(Introduction), 273 III(22)
contagious disease	390,394 IV(33)
containerized traffic	290 III(24)
controlled delivery	Title,249,250,251,252 III(18), 321 III(27)
controlled substances	170 II(11), 182,184,187 II(13), 250 III(18), 321,323 III(27)
corruption	223 III(Introduction), 239,240 III(17)
criminal activities	10 Introduction, 20,22 I(Introduction), 231,241 III(17)
criminal justice system	227 III(Introduction), 397 IV(34)
criminal law	273 III(22)
crop substitution	204 II(15), 211,212,214,218,219,220,221,222 II(16)

Keyword	Paragraph, chapter (target)
customs	43,54 I(2), 92 I(5), 165 II(10), 175,177,179 II(12), 227 III(Introduction), 277 III(22), 289,291,293,294,297,301 III(24), 308,309,311 III(26), 321,322,324 III(27), 341 IV(29)
data	
on demand	25 I(Introduction), 26,27,29,33,35,37,40,41 I(1), Title,44,45,46,50,51 I(2), 70 I(3)
on supply	129,133 II(8), 146,151,155 II(9), 165 II(10), 192 II(14), 208 II(15), 221 II(16)
on treatment	340,341 IV(29), 354 IV(30), 390,392 IV(33), 399,402 IV(34), 420 IV(35)
demography	29 I(1)
dependence-producing potential	131 II(8)
"designer" drugs	182 II(13)
detoxification	88 I(5), 364,368,371 IV(31)
diplomatic status	248 III(17)
disabled	97 I(6)
dispensing practices	149 II(9)
diversion	18 I(Introduction), 123,127 II(Introduction), 160 II(10)
draft convention	180 II(12), 223 III(Introduction)
drug addiction	31 I(1), 127 II(Introduction), 334,335,336,337 IV(Introduction), 338,339,341,344,346 IV(29), 357,359,360 IV(30), 368,376 IV(31), 380,388 IV(32), 399,400,402 IV(34), 408,409,425 IV(35)
drug misuse	Title,27 I(1)
drug therapy	143,148 II(9)
drug-free life-style	58,60 I(3), 108 I(7), 364 IV(31)
drug-related diseases	341 IV(29), 372 IV(31)
early warning	33 I(1), 46 I(2)
economic assistance	188 II(14), 199,203,206 II(15)
economic union	Title,306 III(25)
education	14 Introduction, 24 I(Introduction), 48,49,55 I(2), Title,56,57,58,59,60,61,62,65,67,68,70,71,73 I(3), 85,87,88,91,92,95 I(5), 110,115 I(7), 157 II(9), 203 II(15), 212,214 II(16), 341 IV(29), 366 IV(31), 379 IV(32), 396,404 IV(34), 415,418 IV(35)
emergency relief	160 II(10)
employment	48 I(2), 60 I(3), 83 I(4), 98 I(6), 341 IV(29), 410,419,420,422,424 IV(35)

Keyword	Paragraph, chapter (target)
epidemiological (studies, surveys)	28,29,38,42 I(1), 45 I(2), 357 IV(30)
equipment	
for illicit production	Title,173,174,175,177,178 II(12), 273 III(22), 300 III(24)
for detection	197 II(14), 206 II(15), 296 III(24), 309 III(26)
eradication	18 I(Introduction), 125 II(Introduction), 199,200,202,203,204,205,206,209 II(15), 218 II(16)
essential narcotic drugs	143 II(9)
estimate (legitimate needs)	124 II(Introduction), 128,129 II(8), 158 II(10)
evidence	143 II(9), 158 II(10), 238,241,248 III(17), 257,258,265 III(20), Title,268 III(21), 275 III(22), 284 III(23), 369 IV(31)
export	159,160,161,162 II(10), 174,177 II(12), 188 II(14), 212,217 II(16), 223 III(Introduction), 300 III(24)
extradition	227 III(Introduction), Title,253,254,255,256 III(19)
family	31 I(1), 48 I(2), 56 I(3), 65,67 I(3), 92 I(5), 336 IV(Introduction), 370,372,373 IV(31), 394 IV(33), 418,423,425 IV(35)
farmers	196 II(14), 211,215 II(16)
forfeiture	275 III(22), Title,278,280,286 III(23)
freedom of speech	106 I(7)
freedom of trade	165 II(10)
glossary of terms	360 IV(30)
guidelines	
for prevention	78,84 I(4), 102 I(6), 107 I(7)
for control of supply	128 II(8), 149 II(9)
for law enforcement	252 III(18), 297 III(24)
for treatment	366,367 IV(31), 385 IV(32), 394 IV(33), 402,407 IV(34), 417,426 IV(35)
health	14,17 Introduction, 19 I(Introduction), 27,29 I(1), 48,49 I(2), 58,60,66,67,73 I(3), 85,90,91,92 I(5), 100 I(6), 108,110,112,115,116 I(7), 127 II(Introduction), 131,135,137,142 II(8), 143,146,147,148,149,150,153,157 II(9), 168,170,171 II(11), 182 II(13), 212 II(16), 334,336 IV(Introduction), 338,340,341 IV(29), 350,351 IV(30), 364,365,370,371,374 IV(31), 379,387 IV(32), 389,390,391,393 IV(33), 402 IV(34), 415,420 IV(35)
hepatitis	341 IV(29), 389 IV(33)
herbicide	199,201,202,208 II(15)
heroin	124 II(Introduction)

Keyword	Paragraph, chapter (target)
high seas	Title,326 III(28)
hospital	27,29 I(1), 43 I(2), 129,135 II(8), 420 IV(35)
human right	106 I(7), 265 III(20)
hypnotic	166 II(11)
illicit cultivation	192,195,197,198 II(14), 206,207,208 II(15), 211,212,213,217,219 II(16), 288 III(23)
illicit demand	8,11,15 Introduction, 20,21,22,24,25 I(Introduction), 31,33 I(1), 48 I(2), 68,71 I(3), 90 I(5), 109,116 I(7), 124 II(Introduction), 222 II(16), 224 III(Introduction), 403 IV(34)
illicit laboratories	173 II(12)
illicit production	6,8 Introduction, 58 I(3), 190 II(14), 247 III(17), 269 III(21), 273 III(22)
illicit supply	15 Introduction, 18,21,22 I(Introduction), 224,225 III(Introduction), 284 III(23), 305 III(24)
import	6 Introduction, 135,142 II(8), 152 II(9), 158,159,162,163 II(10), 171 II(11), 175 II(12), 217 II(16), 223 III(Introduction), 273 III(22)
in-patient treatment	370 IV(31)
industrial development	214 II(16)
integrated rural development (IRD)	221 II(16)
international airspace	Title,326 III(28)
international mail	Title,321,322,325 III(27)
International Register on Potentially Toxic Chemicals (IRPTC)	208 II(15)
judicial assistance	227 III(Introduction), 258 III(20)
labelled (pharmaceuticals)	152 II(9)
laboratories	81,84 I(4), 152 II(9), 173 II(12), 257 III(20), 266,268,269 III(21)
laundering (of proceeds)	238 III(17), 273 III(22), 279,287,288 III(23)
law enforcement	14 Introduction, 27 I(1), 54 I(2), Title,85,86,92,95 I(5), 149 II(9), 167 II(11), 173,174,175,179 II(12), 191,193 II(14), 199,200 II(15), 211 II(16), 223,227 III(Introduction), 231,232,234,238,239,242,245 III(17), 249,252 III(18), 257,263 III(20), 266 III(21), 287 III(23), 289 thru 297,303,305 III(24), 307 III(25), 309,312 thru 315,318 III(26), 322 III(27), 328 III(28), 338,341 IV(29)

Keyword	Paragraph, chapter (target)
legal assistance	Title,257,259,262 III(20)
legalization	105 I(7)
legitimate commerce	173 II(12)
legitimate medical (needs, purposes)	6 Introduction, 128,129 II(8), 147,150,156 II(9)
leisure time	60 I(3), 97 I(6)
licit cultivation	124 II(Introduction),
licit production	6 Introduction
literacy programmes	115 I(7), 203 II(15)
major trafficking networks	Title III(17)
manufacture	6 Introduction, 18 I(Introduction), 92 I(5), 123,124,126,127 II(Introduction), 128,135,142 II(8), 158 II(10), 171 II(11), 173,175 II(12), 184,186 II(13), 194 II(14), 270 III(21), 273 III(22), 288 III(23), 300 III(24)
manufacturers	129 II(8), 146,153 II(9), 174 II(12), 395 IV(33)
master plans	207 II(15)
media	78,83 I(4), Title,105,106,107,108,109,110,112,113,114,116,119,120 I(7), 154 II(9)
medical association	43 I(2)
medicament	127 II(Introduction), 160 II(10), 168 II(11), 276 III(22), 370 IV(31)
narcotic drugs	8,17 Introduction, 24 I(Introduction), 58 I(3), 105 I(7), 123,127 II(Introduction), Title,128,129,135,136 II(8), Title,143,145,148,150,152,153,157 II(9), 173,175,180 II(12), 181 II(13), 228 III(Introduction), 267 III(21), 273 III(22), 398 IV(34)
nation-wide strategy	15 Introduction
national focal point	36 I(1)
national legislation	29 I(1), 91 I(5), 135 II(8), 227 III(Introduction), 255 III(19), 280 III(23), 374 IV(31)
national policy	88 I(5), 341,346 IV(29), 402 IV(34)
non-governmental organization	12 Introduction, 24 I(Introduction), 39 I(1), 53 I(2), 68,70,71 I(3), 82 I(4), 94,96 I(5), 111,119 I(7), 132 II(8), 227 III(Introduction), 339 IV(29), 353,354,357 IV(30), 377 IV(31), 385 IV(32), 401 IV(34), 425,427 IV(35)
nosology	27 I(1), 348 IV(29)

Keyword	Paragraph, chapter (target)
offence	18 I(Introduction), 113 I(7), 184 II(13), 227 III(Introduction), 238,239,240 III(17), 253,254,255,256 III(19), 257,258,265 III(20), 266 III(21), 271,272,273,274,275 III(22), 278,282 III(23), 299 III(24), 334 IV(Introduction), 397,398,400,401,403 IV(34)
opiate	124,126 II(Introduction), 188 II(14)
opium poppy	124,125 II(Introduction), 188,191,192 II(14), 199,203,206 II(15), 217,219 II(16)
organized crime	223 III(Introduction)
out-patient treatment	370 IV(31)
parents	12 Introduction, 60,62,64,65 I(3), 89 I(5), 112 I(7), 336 IV(Introduction), 418 IV(35)
patterns (of drug abuse)	27,29,32,34,35,41 I(1), 46 I(2), 111 I(7), 367 IV(31)
penal provision	Title,271 III(22)
penal sanction	18 I(Introduction), 239 III(17)
pharmaceutical industry	49 I(2), 128,129,131 II(8), 149,154 II(9)
pharmacies	134,135 II(8), 147 II(9)
pharmacist	49 I(2), 60 I(3), 129,134 II(8), 149 II(9), 276 III(22)
plantation	190,193,198 II(14), 199,203,206,208 II(15)
police	29 I(1), 43,54 I(2), 66,68 I(3), 92 I(5), 227 III(Introduction), 277 III(22), 308 III(26)
poly-drug use	367 IV(31)
poppy straw	124 II(Introduction), 188 II(14)
possession	27 I(1), 273 III(22), 298 III(24)
precursor	165 II(10), Title,173,174,177 II(12), 292 III(24)
pregnancy	29 I(1), 118 I(7), 367 IV(31)
prescription	92 I(5), 98 I(6), 128 II(8), 144,147,149 II(9), 276 III(22)
prescription drugs	92 I(5), 98 I(6)
prevention of crime	405 IV(34)
prevention strategies	29 I(1)
primary health care	147,148,149 II(9), 338 IV(29), 350 IV(30), 365 IV(31), 387 IV(32)
prison	29 I(1), 274 III(22), 383 IV(32), Title,397,400,401 IV(34),
prisoners' aid	425 IV(35)
privacy	29 I(1), 234 III(17)
production	6,8,9 Introduction, 18 I(Introduction), 58 I(3), 122 I(7), 123,124,126 II(Introduction), 129 II(8), 188,190 II(14), 221,222 II(16), 247 III(17), 269 III(21), 272,273 III(22)

Keyword	Paragraph, chapter (target)
professional associations	12 Introduction, 79 I(4), 89 I(5), 131 II(8)
psychotherapeutic (treatment)	366,372 IV(31)
psychotropic substances	8,17 Introduction, 18,24 I(Introduction), 58,67 I(3), 105 I(7), 127 II(Introduction), Title,128,129,131,135,136 II(8), Title,143,144 thru 148,150 thru 153,156, 157 II(9), Title,158,160,162 thru 165 II(10), Title,168,171 II(11), 173,175,180 II(12), 181 II(13), 228 III(Introduction), 267,268 III(21), 273 III(22), 321 III(27), 396,398 IV(34)
quality control	152 II(9)
rational prescribing	157 II(9)
rational use	Title,146,151,157 II(9)
recidivism	363 IV(31), 414 IV(35)
refugees	73 I(3)
rehabilitation	11 Introduction, 88 I(5), 274 III(22), Title,335,336,337 IV(Introduction), 345 IV(29), Title,349,352,358,361 IV(30), 364,369,371,378 IV(31), 382,387 IV(32), 396,398,406 IV(34), Title,409,410,414,416,417,418,422 IV(35)
religious groups	89 I(5), 417 IV(35)
research	
institutions of research	14 Introduction, 32 I(1), 49 I(2), 128 II(8), 151 II(9), 272 III(22), 280 III(23), 340 IV(29), 401 IV(34)
research on drug abuse	15 Introduction, 27,28,29 I(1), 46,47,48,55 I(2), 68 I(3), 106,111 I(7), 155 II(9), 343 IV(29), 357 IV(30), 365 IV(31)
medical research	131 II(8), 166 II(11), 181,184 II(13)
agricultural research	212,214 II(16)
risk group	98 I(6), 357 IV(30)
rural development assistance	196 II(14)
rural population	125 II(Introduction), 195 II(14), 217 II(16)
safety of the public	81 I(4)
schedules	148 II(9), 158,159,160,161 II(10), 166,167,170,172 II(11)
school	29 I(1), 43 I(2), 59,60,61,62,63,64 I(3), 114 I(7), 203 II(15), 274 III(22), 370 IV(31), 411,412 IV(35)
seizure	105 I(7), 173 II(12), 227 III(Introduction), 237 III(17), 257 III(20), Title,266,267,270 III(21), 278,280,286 III(23), 290 III(24), 329,331 III(28)
self-help associations	338 IV(29), 374 IV(31)
sensing equipment	296 III(24)

Keyword	Paragraph, chapter (target)
social reintegration	8 Introduction, 336 IV(Introduction), 349 IV(30), 362 IV(31), 396 IV(34), Title,416,427 IV(35)
social security	29 I(1), 130,134 II(8)
social welfare	14 Introduction, 29 I(1), 48 I(2), 343 IV(29), 366,370 IV(31), 415 IV(35)
special administration	16 Introduction
specific chemical	Title,173,177 II(12), 292 III(24)
sporting	97,101,103 I(6)
spraying	200,201,202,206,208 II(15)
standardized (data collection)	41 I(1), 45,50 I(2)
statistical (data)	25 I(Introduction), 28,29,33 I(1), 341 IV(29), 402 IV(34)
student	60,62,64 I(3)
substitute crop	192 II(14), 204 II(15), 212,217 II(16)
substitutes (for narcotic drugs)	124 II(Introduction), 363 IV(31)
supply of drugs	18,21 I(Introduction), 123 II(Introduction), 214 II(16), 284 III(23), 305 III(24)
synthetic medicament	127 II(Introduction)
teacher	60,61,62,66,68 I(3), 89 I(5), 112 I(7), 383 IV(32)
terminology	27 I(1), 105 I(7), 360 IV(30)
therapeutic communities	363 IV(31)
tobacco	17 Introduction
tourism	102 I(6), 302 III(24)
traditional use (of coca leaves)	189 II(14)
training	
in prevention	29,38,41 I(1), 61,62,63,64,66,68,69 I(3), 77,82 I(4), 121 I(7)
in control of supply	157 II(9), 175,179 II(12), 215 II(16)
in law enforcement	232,235,238,245 III(17), 252 III(18), 264 III(20), 287 III(23), 295,297 III(24), 312,320 III(26)
in treatment	359 IV(30), 369 IV(31), Title,379,380,381,382,383,385,386,387,388 IV(32), 410,413,419,426 IV(35)
tranquillizer	166 II(11)
transit	165 II(10), 263 III(20), 269 III(21), 293 III(24), 321,322 III(27),
transit countries	165 II(10)
transitional economic assistance	188 II(14), 199,203,205,206 II(15)

Keyword	Paragraph, chapter (target)
transport	102 I(6), 210 II(16), 231,236,237 III(17), 250 III(18), 290,294,297,301 III(24), 312 III(26), 326,332 III(28)
transport companies	237 III(17)
travel agencies	102 I(6)
treatment and rehabilitation techniques	361 IV(30)
trust fund	286 III(23)
unemployment	98 I(6)
university	272 III(22), 280 III(23), 379 IV(32)
urban	5 Introduction, 67 I(3), 373 IV(31)
vessel	293 III(24), 309 III(26), 326,327,328,329,330,331 III(28)
voluntary measures psychotropic substances	127 II(Introduction), 161 II(10)
vulnerable population group	25 I(Introduction), 72 I(3)
women	37 I(1), 118 I(7), 221 II(16), 400 IV(34)
workplace	29 I(1), Title,74,75,76,77,78,83 I(4), 421 IV(35)
young	15 Introduction, 57,60,65,67,73 I(3), 97 I(6), 118 I(7), 419 IV(35)

B. List of organizations

Organization	*Paragraph, chapter (target)*

Centre for Social Development and Humanitarian Affairs
405 IV(34)

Commission on Narcotic Drugs
170 II(11), 176 II(12), 186,187 II(13), 193 II(14),
207 II(15), 228 III(Introduction), 261 III(20),
320 III(26)

Customs Co-operation Council (CCC)
54 I(2), 95 I(5), 177,179 II(12), 245,246 III(17),
252 III(18), 287 III(23), 297,302,304 III(24), 320 III(26),
321 III(27)

Division of Narcotic Drugs
39,40 I(1), 50 I(2), 84 I(4), 137 II(8), 163 II(10),
171 II(11), 179 II(12), 187 II(13), 207 II(15), 245 III(17),
252 III(18), 269 III(21), 287 III(23), 303 III(24),
354 IV(30)

Economic and Social Council
9 Introduction, 53 I(2), 161 II(10), 176 II(12)

Food and Agriculture Organization of the United Nations (FAO)
202,208 II(15), 221 II(16)

Inter-Parliamentary Union
95 I(5)

International Air Transport Association (IATA)
297,302,304 III(24), 320 III(26)

International Association of Ports and Harbors
304 III(24)

International Chamber of Shipping
297,302,304 III(24)

International Civil Aviation Organization (ICAO)
302,304 III(24), 320 III(26)

International Criminal Police Organization (ICPO/Interpol)
54 I(2), 95 I(5), 164 II(10), 179 II(12),
242,245,246 III(17), 252 III(18), 287 III(23),
304 III(24), 320 III(26)

International financing institutions
218 II(16)

International Labour Organisation (ILO)
82,83,84 I(4), 357,358,361 IV(30), 377 IV(31), 426 IV(35)

International Maritime Organization (IMO)
302,304 III(24), 320 III(26)

International Narcotics Control Board (INCB)

    128,137,140,141   II(8),   163,164   II(10),   171   II(11), 174,178 II(12)

regional commissions

    37   I(1),   72   I(3),   221   II(16),   332   III(28),   345   IV(29), 376 IV(31), 387 IV(32)

United Nations Educational, Scientific and Cultural Organization (UNESCO)

    70 I(3), 83 I(4), 119 I(7), 358 IV(30)

United Nations Environment Programme (UNEP)

    208 II(15)

United Nations Fund for Drug Abuse Control (UNFDAC or Fund)

    41   I(1),   71   I(3),   163   II(10),   171   II(11),   195,197   II(14), 207,208,209   II(15),   216,221,222   II(16),   252   III(18), 263   III(20),   269   III(21),   287   III(23),   303   III(24), 312 III(26), 357,358 IV(30)

United Nations Social Defence Research Institute

    405,407 IV(34)

Universal Postal Union (UPU)

    304 III(24), 321,324 III(27)

World Health Organization (WHO)

    27,30,39,40,41,42   I(1),   43,50   I(2),   84   I(4), 128,137,140,142   II(8),   143,147,151,155,157   II(9), 166,169,170,171,172   II(11),   186   II(13),   208   II(15), 344,346,347,348   IV(29), 351,353,354,355,356,357,358,360,361   IV(30), 365,375,376,377   IV(31),   387,388   IV(32), 392,393,394 IV(33), 405,407 IV(34)

World Tourism Organization (WTO)

    302,304 III(24)